The Art of Human Living

The Art of Human Living

MICHAEL H. MITIAS

WIPF & STOCK · Eugene, Oregon

THE ART OF HUMAN LIVING

Copyright © 2025 Michael H. Mitias. All rights reserved. Except for brief quotations in critical publications or reviews, no part of this book may be reproduced in any manner without prior written permission from the publisher. Write: Permissions, Wipf and Stock Publishers, 199 W. 8th Ave., Suite 3, Eugene, OR 97401.

Wipf & Stock
An Imprint of Wipf and Stock Publishers
199 W. 8th Ave., Suite 3
Eugene, OR 97401

www.wipfandstock.com

PAPERBACK ISBN: 979-8-3852-5602-0
HARDCOVER ISBN: 979-8-3852-5603-7
EBOOK ISBN: 979-8-3852-5604-4

VERSION NUMBER 09/03/25

Contents

CHAPTER ONE
Introduction | 1

CHAPTER TWO
A Conception of Human Nature | 8

CHAPTER THREE
The Need for an Art of Human Living | 46

CHAPTER FOUR
A Life Worth Living as Art | 75

CHAPTER FIVE
Artistic Creation and Self-Creation | 106

Suggested References and Bibliography | 137

Index | 139

CHAPTER ONE

Introduction

THE MEANING OF HUMAN LIFE

Directly or indirectly, three fundamental questions underlie the way human beings plan and seek to realize their life projects: How should I live? How should I love? How should I die? Regardless of how they answer them—silently or loudly, thoughtfully or thoughtlessly, wisely or foolishly, critically or naively, independently or dependently—an answer to these questions functions as an irresistible driving force in the decisions they make about the course they take or the attitudes they assume toward the meaning of life. Although these questions express three ways of acting in the world, or three aspects of human existence—namely, living, loving, and dying—they are intimately interrelated mainly because they imply each other logically and existentially. The question of how I should live is inseparable from the question of how I should love. Is the way I love, which is a primary value in human life, not the basic principle of how I should live? Again, the question of how I should face my impending, inevitable death is inseparable from the question of how I should live. Does the consciousness that my life is short make a difference in how I organize the course of my life? But what is the meaning of human life? What makes my life worth living? Is it not worth living? It seems that an adequate, or least reasonable, answer to the three questions about human living should proceed from an adequate, or reasonable, answer to the question of the meaning of human life. Living and dying without knowing or being aware of why or how we should live in this short life of ours, the way the lion roams the wild or the way the bee sucks the nectar of a jasmine flower, or to drift in the forest of human existence aimlessly, is not only a sad, tragic loss of the gift of humanity but also an admission of self-abnegation, which is a clear case of human abortion.

However, it is difficult, indeed undesirable, for humans to live and die without grappling with the question of the meaning of human existence, which includes the questions of living and dying, for two main reasons: first, unlike lions and bees, human beings are self-conscious beings, and second, the human essence (the mind, reason)—that which makes people human beings—is not given to the world as a ready-made reality but, as I shall discuss in this book in some detail, as a reality to be made in the process of daily living. Their lives are not governed by the laws of nature but by laws that emanate from the essential structure of the human essence, although these laws are not inconsistent with the laws of nature. This point calls for the following comments.

The consciousness of the question of the meaning of human life, or the need to ask "how should I live, love, and die?," may be submerged in the tumult of social existence, cultural poverty, narcissistic tendencies, or social and political oppression, but first, no matter the crushing or overwhelming influence of these and similar factors, the impulse to wonder about or confront this central question of the meaning of human life surges into the sphere of human consciousness in moments of distress, failure, triumph, joy, devastating sickness, elation, or especially when we approach the last edge of life. Do we not frequently hear people who retire and then feel the sting of loneliness, boredom, or waning physiological and psychological strength say, "Life sucks," "I wish I could live my life all over again," or "I did not know that death has been waiting for me around the corner! I wish I could live my life backward!"? Even the confession of a mature person that their life was good and worth living, or that they are not afraid of their imminent death, betrays a consciousness of the question of the meaning of human life.

Second, in all its manifestations in the world, the human essence does not exist as a natural or sensuously perceptible reality the way plants, rocks, and animals do. We do not encounter an object we can call or identify as "human essence," "human mind," or "human nature" anywhere in the realm of nature or the social marketplace. To borrow a metaphor from Plato, that which transforms a biped into a human being "dwells" in the human body. But a close look at the mode of this dwelling will show that the human essence does not exist in any organ of the body or as an identifiable part of it;

Introduction

its existence is omnipresent, that is, immanent, in every fiber of its being. It is what makes the body shine with the radiance of human essence. A body that does not speak the language of the human essence is not a human body. But if human essence does not exist in the body as a physical element of its constitution, how does it come to life as a subject that presides over a human individual? What is its source? Can we understand its nature if we do not know its source? How can a nonphysical reality inhabit and pervade a physical reality like the human body? It is, I submit, reasonable to argue, as I shall do, that the human body emerges as a unique reality from the cosmic process, that it is unique by virtue of its capacity to possess the human essence, that this essence exists as a potentiality in the formal organization of the human body, and that it comes to life in a state of self-consciousness. Moreover, as a potentiality, the human essence is a possibility for inexhaustible realizations in different ways and forms. Accordingly, the life of a human being consists of such realizations. The human being is not a ready-made reality but a reality to be made and, more concretely, a reality to be created in the process of realizing one's life project. The human being is essentially a self-created being. Every new moment of human development opens new possibilities for more substantial realizations. This assertion sheds light on the generally recognized principle in ethical theory that the destiny of the human being consists of a continual process of growth and development, or perfection. Implied in this thread of reasoning is that the human essence is neither a physical nor a metaphysical entity in the ways Plato, Descartes, and many of the classical thinkers held but a reality in a constant state of self-creation. This assertion is founded on the fundamental assumption that in all its manifestations, the essence of cosmic reality is not only a process but a creative advance.

METHODOLOGY

The first two chapters aim to provide the groundwork for a conception of authentic human life as an art. I am anxious to obviate the pitfall of naive subjectivism or relativism. The logical insight that prompts, indeed necessitates, this methodological step is the fact the principles according to which human beings can lead a life worth living cannot be based on a subjective, weak, soft, or shaky foundation. Leading such a life is, I believe, the most important ideal that illuminates the road that leads to human growth and development, individually and communally. We can sometimes afford to make a mistake, embark on an adventure we deem significant, and wager on the viability, worthwhileness, or merit of the possibility of a project in our social or professional life, but we cannot afford to wager or be uncertain or vague about the logical and practical firmness of the ground on which we stand in our endeavor to leading a justifiable or worthwhile life. Do religious people not stand on the ground of faith as the basis for believing in a god they cannot conceive or experience? Do we not do our best to make sure to endeavor to meet the right person to be our spouse, that they are loving and honorable without a shred of doubt? Although the quest for certainty in the pursuit of knowledge, which has been an established orientation, almost a dogma, ever since the rise of human civilization, may be undermined by the unprecedented developments of science and philosophy in the first half of the last century, the need for certainty in everything we do in our lives remains strong, a practical demand. Living in uncertainty is a serious source of anxiety, fear, and cynicism. This need figures prominently in our endeavor to lead a meaningful or happy life.

The groundwork, whose structure I shall analyze and use as a principle of explanation in the remainder of the book, is based on the most recent findings in neurology, physics, and extensive studies in the philosophy of mind during the past few decades. I have endeavored to articulate the fundamental insight of these three sources into a viable conception of human nature. An insight is "the ability to see or understand the inner nature of things."[1] The ability to have an insight is often acquired through intuition. Intuition is a direct or immediate comprehension, grasp, or knowing of the nature of reality without the aid of reasoning, concepts, or images. Its meaning can be communicated by different types of symbolic forms—conceptual, acoustic, pictorial, active, plastic, or imagistic. I have delved deep into the meaning implicit in the latest discoveries in physics, neurology, and philosophical studies. I have adapted the concepts of "cosmic process" from physics, "human essence" from neuroscience, and "mind" from philosophy. It is clear that this interdisciplinary methodological step is based on the firm belief that types of human knowledge are organically interrelated primarily because they are of different dimensions of the same world of which human beings are integral parts.

---

1. *Webster's New World College Dictionary.*

Introduction

THESIS

The question of how I should live, love, and die streams into human consciousness from the womb of a more urgent question of the meaning of human life: What makes my life worth living? Is the life I have led, or am still leading, justifiable? This question demands an answer for five main reasons—first, because I do not exist in the world as a ready-made reality the way natural objects do. Accordingly, my life as a human reality is not directly governed by the laws of nature the way the life of natural objects is governed but as a continual process of realization. The "I" that presides over the course of my life is a dynamic reality and appears in my consciousness as a power that authors the designs and implementation of every action I perform in the course of my daily life. I cannot, no matter how much I try, capture or grasp this "I" as an entity. I feel its existence as a continual process in action. I apprehend myself at once as this process and as the subject that presides over its activities. Second, the natural and social world in which I am anchored is a thrust into the future—the next second, minute, day, week, month, year, or century. My past lingers in my present state of being, and my future emanates from my present state of being. The future is forbidden to my intellectual eyes. I can, on the basis of past experience, envision what my life will be like in the next moment in the near or foreseeable future, but I cannot envision clearly and with certainty what will happen in the distant future, even if I plan it clearly. The next moment of my life is always vitiated with an underlying streak of hope, possibility, uncertainty, and contingency. Third, even though I am not aware of it, I accept the fact that I am a creature, in the sense that I and my parents are created by a superior power, one I cannot comprehend. When I reach the highest point of my adolescence, I discover that I exist, that my reality is single or individual, and that I am different from any human or natural object around me. I also discover that I did not choose to be born, as if some power placed in this particular corner of the universe. Neither did my parents! Perhaps they chose my existence but not my kind of existence! Ontologically, I do not know why I was created. Gradually, I discovered that not only I but all the physical, botanical, and animal objects, all human beings, are processes—an ongoing process of change that will sooner or later cease to exist. This twofold discovery amounts to a realization that my life is short. Fourth, and a corollary to the preceding discovery, I gradually recognize that, unlike natural projects, I am a self-conscious being. I do not only exist; I know that I exist, and I can be conscious of myself as an object to myself. Moreover, I know that I am, in principle, the sole author of my life. My consciousness does not have doors, windows, or any holes. No one can feel my feelings, think my thoughts, or act on my behalf. Therefore, I am responsible for how I should live. Implicit in this responsibility is that I possess a sense of value—of goodness, beauty, love, grandeur, justice, truth, and a multitude of similar values. Fifth, as I grow up and develop as a human being and acquire an intense feeling of self-consciousness, I discern that I am important, not only because I know that I exist as a special kind of being, which is a privilege, but especially because, in contrast to any object around me, I can choose to act according to laws inherent in my nature as a human individual. The capacity of self-creation implies a sense of importance, and the sense of importance implies the ability to discriminate and evaluate. I can distinguish between the good and the bad, the beautiful and the ugly, the appropriate and the inappropriate, the grand and the mediocre, the admirable and the disgusting, the desirable and the undesirable, the sacred and the profane. Sixth, it becomes clear to me when I leave the mentality of adolescence behind and charge into the world of maturity, which is crowded with loud, and sometimes silent, quizzical questions, feelings, attitudes, and situations, that in fact I have three legs: the first standing in the past, the second standing in the present, and the third standing in the future. And I have three faces: the first sees the past, the second sees the present, and the third sees future. Although I exist in the present moment, although the domain of this moment is opaque, porous, and often vague, I practically live in the future. This existential consciousness can be articulated in the form of a question: What should I do in the next moment—minute, hour, day, week, next year, or the rest of my life? Alas! How can I think of the next moment, no matter its length or area of experience, if my life needs to be created in every new moment and if it does not originate from a life project I have designed and developed with the help of my parents and society or by imitating a person I trust and respect such as a friend, teacher, historical luminary, or sage?

The thesis I shall advance, elaborate on, and defend in this book is that living, loving, and dying competently, wisely, and justifiably is an art. Implied in this thesis is the fundamental and unquestionable assumption that (1) human life is a process of continual self-creation, (2) it derives its being and logic of creation from the human essence, (3) it is true to the demands and aspirations of the human essence, and (4) its substance consists of an ongoing activity of self-realization or self-perfection. Only a life that

Introduction

flows from the mind and heart of the human individual to these demands and aspirations is justifiable. Such a life does not fear death and does not quake when it approaches the last line of its existence but, on the contrary, welcomes it contentedly and peacefully. This line of reasoning is based on the six existential aspects of human existence I discussed in the preceding paragraph.

My attempt to establish the validity of my thesis will, first, proceed from an adequate, or at least a reasonable, conception of human nature. This conception should include an analysis of the elements or powers that make people human realities in contrast to every other type of reality in the cosmic process: the structure of the human essence. What are the dynamics of this essence? What are its drives, capacities, and goals? Under what conditions can these goals be realized? In what sense is their fulfillment the source of human happiness or human perfection? The second requisite for establishing the validity of my thesis is an elucidation of the concept of art: What is art? In what sense is the life of a human being art? How can skill in this art be cultivated? I shall illustrate the proposition that the human being is a self-created being, that their life is a continual process of self-creation, and that this activity is artistic by a detailed analysis of three basic types of human experience: loving, teaching, and practical vocation or profession. In what follows, I shall present a chapter-by-chapter description establishing the validity of my thesis.

CHAPTER TWO

A Conception of Human Nature

THE QUESTION OF HUMAN NATURE

I submit that the construction of an adequate conception of human nature should begin with an explanation of the genesis of the element, power, or phenomenon whose presence in the human body transforms it into a human reality: What is human nature? What do we have in mind when we speak of human nature or when we say that human beings are, by nature, rational, good, selfish, social, or religious? Is human nature a unique type of reality? How does it exist in the human body if it is a reality? What is its structure? Can it be a reality if it does not have a structure? When I interact with a human being socially, politically, religiously, intellectually, or romantically, do I interact with a lump of flesh or a lump of human flesh? If this lump is human, what makes it human? Can it be a direct object of perception or reflection, like rocks and trees? Again, how can we make any assertion about its existence or the kind of reality it is if we cannot either perceive it or reflect on it as a reality?

In my endeavor to answer these and related questions, I shall sidestep the plethora of views advanced by philosophers since the days of Plato and Aristotle to the present. However, I shall not in any way ignore them or the insight they express. On the contrary, I shall begin where they left off. The conception of human nature I shall advance will be based on the most recent findings of neuroscience and philosophy of mind. I shall argue that, although it does not exist as a discrete or independent object, human nature is a phenomenon that comes into being in the medium of human experience as a spiritual reality. I shall begin the development of my argument with some historical and methodological observations. The proposition I shall present and defend is that any discourse about human nature is a discourse about the human essence as a phenomenon that emerges from the cosmic process with the emergence of the human body and that this essence exists as a potentiality in the formal organization of the human body. Accordingly, although it does not exist as a discrete or independent object, in the realm of nature, the way trees or animals exist, we can experience and examine its reality in and through its manifestations in the world: human subjectivity, living human beings, and the realm of human civilization. This assertion is based on the assumption that we know a reality by its effects or role in its environment. Similarly, we know a human being by what they do or the actions they perform in the world. In this chapter, I shall conclude my discussion with a detailed analysis of the essential structure of the human essence and the values that emanate from the logic of its dynamics. The insight that underlies this analysis is expressed by Plato's well-known analogy, which he articulated in *The Republic*: society is the human soul writ large. In this analysis, I assume that not only the human essence but also the life of the human individual are the human essence writ large, in the sense that the life of a human being is a concrete realization of the capacities that constitute the essential structure of the human essence. Accordingly, we know what it means for a human being to be a human reality by examining the kinds of activities they perform in the context of their social life.

METHODOLOGICAL AND HISTORICAL ASSUMPTIONS

Ever since the rise of philosophy in the hands of the pre-Socratics, beginning in the seventh century BC, philosophers have been grappling with some of the most difficult questions the human mind can ask: (1) What is the primary cause or creator of the universe? Does such a cause exist? If it does, what kind of being is it? Is it in any way related to human life or to how people should live? (2) What is the nature of the universe; for example, what is the essential nature of matter, life, and consciousness? (3) What is the source of human values; for example, what is the nature of truth, goodness, and beauty? How can we establish the validity of our knowledge of these values? (4) What is the nature of the mind that asks these and many other important questions about cosmic process? (5) How should people live individually and communally? (6) Is there life after death? Although these questions begin with "what is the nature of—" they reflect an urge to know the essential character of the constitutive elements that make up the structure of a reality, regardless of whether it is a rock we see on the side of the road, a bee sucking the nectar of a flower, the sun that illuminates our planet, or the force that energizes the process of motion, life, or human behavior. They exist as objects of perception or interest. They betray the existence of two remarkable powers of the human mind. The first is curiosity, and the second is the desire to survive as human beings. The first is theoretical, and the second is practical. The primary aim of the first is understanding, and the primary aim of the second is human growth and development.

If we reflect and critically examine the traditional territory of philosophical inquiry, we discover that it includes four main areas of investigation: (1) metaphysics, which aims to understand the nature of the universe as an ordered whole, that is, in terms of its source, structure, and significance; (2) epistemology, which aims to investigate the source, nature, and validity of human knowledge and the limits of the cognitive powers of the human mind; (3) axiology, which aims to investigate the source and nature of human values; and (4) logic, which aims to investigate the nature the principles of correct reasoning in the domains of theoretical and practical experience. An answer to these questions is usually articulated into a systematic, rational, and comprehensive conception, or a conceptual framework of the nature of a dimension of human and physical reality. The fundamental intuition underlying the articulation of this conception differs from one philosopher to another and from one ideological, cultural, and historical period to another. Broadly, it functioned as (1) a principle of explanation and (2) a basis of designing individual life projects and sociopolitical policies. The first represents a response to the desire to know or understand the nature of this amazing universe, and the second represents a practical response to the impulse of human survival. As I shall presently explain in detail, these two functions entail each other: knowledge of oneself and the environment in which people live is a necessary condition for appropriating nature to human survival. It was assumed that the conception is a conceptual model of the essential structure of the given natural or human dimension of reality. Penetrating deep into its structure is tantamount to a penetration into the nature of the world and human life. The conception acts as (1) a source of insight or understanding of the cosmic story of the universe, (2) self-understanding, and (3) designing the plan of one's life. Although sketchily, I made this remark to underscore the historical fact that the pursuit of knowledge in all its kinds, regardless of whether it was theoretical or practical, has been the task of the philosopher. All knowledge has been viewed as philosophical knowledge and its attainment the task of the philosopher.

Science was not recognized as a discipline or kind of knowledge until its empirical method of investigating the nature of physical and biological reality was theoretically and practically effective and productive. This moment of recognition was generally acknowledged at the turn of the last century. For example, scientists such as Newton in the eighteenth century viewed themselves as philosophers, and philosophers such as Hegel viewed themselves as scientifically minded thinkers. Again, Descartes was a mathematician, physicist, and philosopher. His *Discourse on Method*, not to mention the work of Roger Bacon, was influential in the rise and development of the scientific method. However, the development of the scientific method of inquiry into the nature of the world as a whole picked up momentum when it became clear that the method of philosophy, which was based on metaphysical principles and assumptions, was deficient in the attempt to study, explain, or comprehend the nature of physical reality, namely, the scheme of nature. This discovery—which was made possible by thinkers such as Tycho Brahe, Kepler, Copernicus, and Galileo, and later by scientists such as Lavoisier and Darwin, was gradual, and reached a high point of development in the second half of the nineteenth century—led to a formal and generally acknowledged difference between science and philosophy. In the study of nature, sense observation replaced metaphysical intuition and assumptions as a basis of knowing the nature of physical objects.

It is important to stress that although science emerged from the womb of philosophy as a distinct method of investigation of physical and biological reality, it has not, contrary to many science enthusiasts, severed its umbilical cord from its mother discipline. It is extremely difficult, and I think impossible, to leave it. The relation between them is intimate, organic. Speculation remains an essential element of scientific thinking, and sensual observation of the scheme of nature remains the fundamental datum of speculation. Neither one is possible without the other. Moreover, this relation was keenly recognized by philosophers and scientists alike at the turn of the twentieth century. For example, philosophers such as Bergson,

Whitehead, and Russell based their systems on the contemporary findings of physical and biological science. They argued that the task of science is to know the nature of reality insofar as it is an object of sensual observation—namely, nature—and the task of the philosopher is to know the nature of the *meaning* of this reality. In all its modes of being, meaning is not, and cannot be, an object of sensory observation. It can be experienced (1) contemplating the scheme of nature as a possible object of observation, the way scientists do, and (2) reflecting on the knowledge achieved by scientists. The task of the philosopher begins when the work (*ergon*) of the scientist ends. For example, the scientist can say that physical and biological reality is a creative advance, the human essence emerges from the formal organization of the human body, or the human body is a unique emergent form of the natural process. These and similar kinds of statements are verifiable empirically. The philosopher can say, What do we mean when we say that biological and physical reality is a creative advance, the human essence emerges from the formal organization of the human body, or the human body is a unique emergent from the natural process? What are the implications of these and similar scientific statements? What is their relevance to human life? I do not know of recent or contemporary philosophers who are not scientifically minded or scientists who are not philosophically minded. I spotlight this point because, unfortunately, many practicing philosophers and scientists do their work as if science is separated from philosophy by a solid wall, as if they are not related, as if they cannot dialogue.

It is obvious that knowledge of the scientist predominates in the rapidly evolving human culture primarily because it is practically useful in three ways: first, as Francis Bacon observed some time ago, knowledge is power; accordingly, knowledge of nature and the dynamics of its processes enable the human mind to appropriate its environment to meet the needs of human and natural survival. Second, scientific knowledge inspires and effectuate the whole world of technology, which has promoted the well-being of people significantly. And third, scientific knowledge is vitally essential to our understanding of human nature, which is a condition for the betterment of human life. At present, physical, biological, and technological knowledge is the foundation of human existence. But although it plays a supremely important role in steering the wheels of civilization, it is not the paradigm of human knowledge because the domain of human reality is wider and, in some cases, superior to the value of natural reality. As I shall discuss in detail, human beings are not merely bodies but human bodies.

A Conception of Human Nature

The human as such is not an integral part of the fabric of nature; it inheres in the formal organization of the human body as a potentiality. It exists in it but thrives in a built (human) environment by (1) transforming nature into a human environment and (2) creating human institutions within which they grow and develop as human individuals. The realm of nature is a realm of what is, or what is given, or what is. The human realm is a realm of what is possible or what can be. This realm is born of the womb of speculation on the basis of sensual observation and supplemented by scientists' knowledge. It may seem strange if I remark in this context that science itself was born from the womb of speculation; it is, after all, a human creation.

ORIGIN OF THE HUMAN PHENOMENON

The "human phenomenon" is distinctive in that it emerges from a particular environment within the vast cosmic processes, yet it grows and develops in a physical environment, which inclines one to think that it came into being *ex nihilo*, for it seems logically difficult for something nonphysical to emerge from something physical. In the amazing diversity of their ways of thinking, people sometimes speak of miracles, and at other times they speak of the miraculous, mainly because the way the human phenomenon exists and flourishes seems to violate, if not transcend, the laws of nature. However, I think it is appropriate to say that if there is anything miraculous in the world so far as we know it, the existence of the human phenomenon, not simply because it emerges from a physical environment but especially because it thrives and constructs an infinitely vast world, uniquely different from the physical environment from which it emerged. The method of science, which adheres strictly to the empirical method of observation in seeking knowledge of nature, does not provide the conditions for investigating the nature of the human phenomenon. It can assert and explain how or why it is an emergent and the extent to which it depends on its physical environment, including the human body, but it cannot judge its essential nature or the laws that govern its continual development or destiny. The philosopher, whose method of inquiry is intuitive, discursive, and speculative, proceeds from a comprehensive knowledge of the nature of our knowledge of the world. The unity of its details, and the dynamic relation between them, can—as I shall momentarily explain—help us comprehend the nature and existence of the human phenomenon. People undertake this kind of inquiry because they can reflect on the nature of the world on the basis of scientific knowledge and a synoptic vision of the philosophical mind, stepping into the domain of the human phenomenon as a living reality. It can do this because the human essence is given as an emergent, the way all emergents are given, but it is not given as a ready-made reality the way rocks, trees, or cats are given. It emerges and consequently exists as a potentiality that is inherently capable of realizing the possibilities in its essential structure. The impulse to achieve biological survival necessarily prompts its emergence. How? The human body is organized in a manner that facilitates its emergence. The conditions of survival of every organism are inherent in its formal organization. Its capacity to survive in a certain environment depends on its capacity to respond to the existing conditions effectively and utilize its resources to survive. The formal organization of the human body inherently possesses the capacity to survive biologically and consequently as a human reality. The emergence of intelligence as a power in its essential structure enables the human body to use the resources of its natural environment to meet the needs of survival.

If, as you posit, the human phenomenon emerges *qua* potentiality as a unique reality, if it is nonphysical and as such cannot be an object of sensuous observation, my critic would now ask, how do we recognize or know it? What is its ontological status? Moreover, what kind of reality is it? We know what it means for something to be a stone, an apple tree, or a lion because they are types of structures or because they are complexes of perceptible qualities. These qualities are the content of our perception. Their mode of formal organization is the basis of their identity. All natural or biological objects are made of the same biological or material stuff—life and matter. They are different, and so are their different identities, by virtue of the fact that their perceptible qualities are organized in a certain way. Form is the medium in which we cognize the nature of an object. However, the human phenomenon is not given as a ready-made, that is, formed, reality but as a potentiality. Does such a potentiality have a formal structure? Do we perceive its structure when we perceive it? Can you shed light on this aspect of the human phenomenon? These are reasonable questions; they are a request to explain the ontological status of the human essence as a potentiality in the formal organization of the human body and the sense in which it is generically different from the nature of physical realities.

The ontic locus of the human phenomenon is the human body. It exists in this kind of body, *qua* biological reality, and nowhere else. It is not one of its given organs. This is why I emphasize that it inheres in its formal organization. Although it inheres in the formal organization of the human body as a whole, the highest concretization of its inherence is concentrated in the brain as the center that regulates the functions of the body.

First, by "human phenomenon," or human essence, I mean what is traditionally known as soul, spirit, mind, reason, and more recently consciousness. I characterize the human essence as a phenomenon to distinguish it from any metaphysical, physical, or psychological kind of reality. That which is human is neither physical nor metaphysical in character; it is not a ready-made or given reality but a "drop" or a "flare" of human life, one that exists as a *lived experience*. This kind of experience is its birthplace and home. Like the cosmic process from which it emerged, it is a process, and unlike any other emergent from this process, it is a self-created reality. As such, it is a center of being. Its existence and life emanate from this center. It exists and endures as long as the center endures. This feature justifies characterizing it as a phenomenon. The word "phenomenon" comes from the Greek *phenomenon*, a preposition of *phainesthai*, "to appear," which is akin to *phainein*, "to see."[1] A phenomenon is an object that exists as a reality, that is, as a particular kind of noetic essence in the medium of human experience, regardless of whether the basis that gives rise to it is physical, psychological, or metaphysical. Moreover, the mode of being of a phenomenon is that of an appearance, not the appearance of a fantastical or phantasmagorical object but the appearance of an essence, that is, a noetic essence that appears to the mind in a special kind of intuition or apprehension. It appears as a flare or a living moment of being. We intuit this kind of flare when we undergo a primary type of human experience—religious, aesthetic, moral, romantic, intellectual, or any of the multitude of human experiences. Broadly, the experience of human presence is an experience of a living moment of the human phenomenon. It is a moment in which human essence comes to life as a flare of human being.

Second, as a living flare of life, the human phenomenon always exists as an *embodied reality*. It does not exist as an independent, single, or discrete reality. Implied in this fact is that we do not encounter it as an object in the scheme of nature, as a mental state in the sphere of mind, or as a metaphysical entity in the mind of the philosopher, scientist, theologian, or artist. However, we encounter it as an object of knowledge and a moment of human existence or life in three kinds of embodiments: first, in their domain of human subjectivity; second, in the living human beings

---

1. *Webster's New World College Dictionary.*

who constitute our social environment; and third, in the whole realm of human civilization, which consists of the achievements of human beings in the course of human history.

First, the domain of subjectivity is the realm of a human being's inner life. It is not physical because it is essentially human, and it is a manifestation of a human life. This realm comes to life in a state of self-consciousness, and it does not exist outside this realm. "Self-consciousness" implies a self, that is, a subject that presides over the life of a human being. It comes into being as a self, that is, as an actor or agent, in this state and cognizes itself as such an actor or agent by (1) recognizing itself as a subject, that is, as the author of its activities, and (2) by recognizing its capacity to choose or consciously author the way it thinks, feels, or makes decisions. This is possible because the self that is conscious of itself as a subject is not an abstract reality but a world of human experience that exists as a manifold of ideas, emotions, beliefs, desires, moods, memories, and a large cluster of similar mental states. Standing before itself in a moment of self-consciousness is, in effect, standing before a stream of human life or before a world of a particular human being. I emphasize this feature of subjectivity only to shed light on the premise that the first mode of human embodiment, namely, subjectivity, is the first and, I can add, paradigmatic source of our knowledge of the human essence. The human world that emerges from the activities of the human essence, which does not exist as an integral part of the scheme of nature, is as real, and I can say more real, than the reality of the natural objects that make up our environment. As I indicated earlier, human beings exist in the realm of nature but thrive in an environment they build. Human subjectivity is the first domain that reveals the essential structure of the human essence. It is important to note that the built environment is not revealed as a physical or psychological object, one that stands before the faculty of perception as a ready-made object because it does not have the nature or character of such an object, but as a noetic essence that comes to life in and through its concrete manifestations in the human and natural realms of being, or in the essential structure in which it inheres as a potentiality. The human as such is always a flare of human experience or life. It is a radiance of human existence. It does not exist outside this radiance.

I made the preceding jaunt into scientific and metaphysical thinking to bring into relief the outline of the method I employ in my attempt to explain the nature of the human essence and the way it manifests itself as a *sui generis* creative power in the world. The first and primary domain in which it manifests itself concretely is human subjectivity, namely, the abundance of mental states we encounter when we turn the eyes of our minds inward: ideas, desires, emotions, and a plethora of feelings and attitudes about objects and situations. They are artifacts because they are human creations and exist exclusively for the subject. Like artifacts such as practical instruments and works of art, they are human embodiments. This is why it is appropriate to treat them as human realities. Insofar as they are stored in the belly of the mind, these states are given. However, they are transformed into human realities when in a thread of thinking or feeling. This givenness defines their character as "states." A state can be defined lexically, stipulatively, idiomatically, conventionally, or practically. These definitions are basic to communication and translation. In this case, the idea is given, albeit psychologically in character, mainly because its signification is defined or articulated. It can be treated as a commodity or as a social, religious, political, or personal "good" or possession. Accordingly, it may exist in the world the way physical objects do because, like physical objects, ideas come into being and pass out of being at different times and places and under certain experiential conditions. But, as given objects, mental states are not, strictly speaking, human objects but artificial objects. They are human embodiments. As such, they exist as potentialities for being human phenomena in the activity of thinking, feeling, and imagining, that is, when the mind apprehends the meaning they signify. In this type of activity, they are transformed from being mental states into being living flares of meaning, which are usually experienced when we can, in principle, say, "I understand! I see the point you are making" or "I got it!" Only when an idea is transformed into a flare of meaning can it be communicated or understood, for otherwise, how can an idea in your mind move into mine or an idea in my mind move into yours? No matter their kind, psychological states are locked up in the domain of subjectivity.

Let me illustrate this point with an example. Suppose I hate Paul because he harmed my son without a justifiable cause or because he committed a capital offence against a member of my family. The emotion of hatred exists in my mind as a mental state. Suppose one day, when I am walking toward a store, I suddenly see Paul walking toward me. In his case, his sight would transform the emotion of hate that exists in my mind as a mental state into a vivid emotion. The emotion that existed in my mind as a potentiality is now an actual, living reality. Again, as a mental state, the emotion exists exclusively in my mind. Does it affect him? Would he know about it? No. He would know about it, or I can communicate it to him by verbal or bodily gesture, in which the meaning implicit in my emotion of hatred springs from my mind as a flare of living meaning. Only then does the state cease to be a state and become a human expression. Human meaning is not a psychological state. It is a mode of existence in which the human essence in its capacity as intellect manifests itself in the world concretely. Like words or any kind of symbolic expression, mental states are vehicles, carriers, shells that convey human meaning. Meaning can be communicated, expressed, or conveyed, but the vehicle or shell cannot. When you speak to me, I understand what you say. What I understand is the meaning of the words you say or utter. When I read a book, do the printed words on paper jump into my mind while I read it? No. Do your words move in my mind when I listen to your speech? No. Regardless of whether they are ideas, emotions, beliefs, or images, mental states are human creations or artifacts, and like all human creations, they are human embodiments. There are always potentialities for realizing deeper and novel human meaning.

Subjectivity is a human embodiment. It is a world of human experience. Every one of its elements is a human embodiment. They function as a mirror in which the human mind sees itself. Their unity is the basis of one's identity as a particular human being. The totality of the experiences that exist in the mind as a conglomeration of mental states, that is, as potentialities—they come to life in two significant moments: first when we are in a state of self-consciousness in which we are engaged in a certain question or problem, and second, in the course of daily living, indirectly when we face these problems. I say indirectly because every experience we undergo in a present moment is realized in terms of the wealth of the mental states that make up the structure of the mind.

As a potentiality, the human essence consists of four primary capacities or powers, namely, intellect, affection, volition, and sensibility. Its emergence is not fortuitous, accidental, or a freaky accident in the cosmic process; on the contrary, it reflects the creative advance of this process, which is a thrust toward higher states of being. As an emergent of this process, the human essence is essentially an impulse to biological and human survival. This twofold impulse is its main mode of being in the world. Here, the question that stares us in the face is, what is the logic that underlies the emergence of the human essence? Or, why does its structure consist of four primary capacities? The essence of the stone is given; its being consists of repeating its essential structure as a lump of matter in every next state of its

A Conception of Human Nature

being as a process. The essence of the lion, which is a higher kind of reality, does not consist merely of repeating the essential structure of its identity as a lump of matter especially as a lump of living matter. It cannot consist of repeating its identity at every next state if its existence because, in addition to being matter, it is also life. The possibility of life exists as a potentiality in the formal organization of its body. Its body is organized in a way that allows for the possibility of the emergence of life. If, for some reason, a lion cannot meet the conditions of living, it will be reduced to a lump of matter and will endure as long as this lump endures. This is why the lion is born with the instinct and means of survival. The logic that underlies its existence, endurance, or life is one and the same everywhere in the universe. The means of endurance of any kind of object are inherent in its formal organization. It ceases to exist when the conditions of its endurance cease to exist.

However, the potentiality of endurance of the human body as a living organism is not given as a ready-made structure the way it is given in animals, plants, or physical objects but as a unique nature, in contrast to any other kind of reality in the natural process. Its mode of existence is that of potentiality. Nonetheless, like every living reality, it exists as an impulse to life—to human life. What does it take for this kind of impulse to be realized concretely in a natural environment? What is the logic that governs the process of its realization?

The logic of its realization inheres directly in the impulse to human life, which includes the impulse to biological survival. This is in contrast to the logic of biological survival in plants and animals, which inheres in the structure of the natural process. The human body does not, by virtue of its formal organization, seek to survive merely as a particular lump of flesh but as a human reality; its quest for survival is a quest for human survival. Securing its survival as a living organism is a means, or a condition, for survival as a human reality primarily because, as a potentiality, the impulse to life is not *merely* an impulse for a reality that is uniquely different from the reality of the human body as a living organism but to exist as an autonomous being, that is, to extricate its being and consequently its life from the strictures of the laws that govern the natural process. The laws that govern its realization are inherent in the structure of the human essence. The secret of this logic lies in the capacity of the human being to be a self-conscious reality. Without this kind of consciousness, it exists as an integral part of the natural process. This capacity enables the developing person to reflect on themself and their environment and assess the means and conditions of their survival. The logical conditions of this possibility imply the existence of four capacities: (1) the design of a human being and the environment in which they exist, (2) the means of realizing the design, (3) the will to initiate the process of realizing it, and (4) the instrumentality by which the process of realization takes place. Put differently, the possibility of survival requires intelligence or imagination, desire or passion, will, and the practical skill by which the natural environment can be utilized in the activity of surviving. If we examine the throng of mental states on the ground on which they stand as rays of being emanating from the human essence, we discover that this ground consists of the primary capacities of intellect, affection, volition, and sensibility. These four capacities underlie the realization of every desire we try to meet, the conception of every goal we aim to realize, the envisioning of every aspiration we hope to achieve, the pursuit of any kind of experience we embark on, and the endeavor to understand any aspect or dimension of human and natural reality. The development of these four capacities as conditions of human survival did not happen overnight, or by the magical power of a supernatural force, or by a freakish accident but by gradual, arduous, and progressive evolution. A philosopher like Hegel would say that this evolutionary development was designed and engineered by the cunning eyes and mind of the power (reason) that steers the cosmic process. One may interpret this possible way of explaining the direction of the cosmic process as optimistic, if not anthropocentric, but regardless of how we explain it, we cannot directly witness or decipher the real spirit of the eyes and mind. We can plausibly assert that our knowledge of the first manifestation of the human essence is human subjectivity primarily because it is the center of creation that gives rise to any kind of human reality insofar as it can be perceived, felt, and understood in the medium of human experience. Undermine human subjectivity, and you *ipso facto* undermine the existence of the human phenomenon in all its manifestations.

The second domain of embodied humanity that can be the source of our knowledge of the human essence, namely, its structure, dynamics, possibilities, and the logic that underlie its growth and development as a unique reality in the world, is the living human, either individually or collectively, in the different spheres of practical and theoretical life. We acquire this knowledge by analogy. The method of acquiring it is by direct, or immediate, interaction with human beings in the different institutions and organizations that make up the structure of society and indirectly by observing their behavior in these institutions and organizations. We know the nature of an organism by what it does or by the effects it produces. It is a generally recognized fact that we know human beings by what they do, not merely by what they think or feel about themselves, although we should not neglect what they think or feel about themselves, mainly because such thoughts and feelings are integral parts of their minds as particular human beings and because every human subjectivity is a human depth, which is sometimes hard for anyone to fathom. Do we not know more, and sometimes exceedingly more, about an artist, scientist, philosopher, or social reformer by discovering their successes, achievements, failures, weaknesses, desires, aspirations, frustrations, hopes, and disappointments? But, generally speaking, the kind of being a person is reveals through their nature as a shining presence in actions, social behavior, or life. A serious reflection on the logic and dynamics of this revelation will, I suggest, disclose not only what the human being has done but also what they can do. The more we delve into what the human essence does or produces, the more we know about what it does, did, and can do. This proposition is based on the fundamental assumption that what we do and how we behave in the world is an objectification of our inner selves. The "I" that exists in the world becomes real in the way it actually lives. The course of life the human being leads, from the moment they come into the world to the moment they leave it, is an objective or macrocosmic mirror of the human actor, or mind, that presides over the design and realization of this macrocosmic mirror.

If we undertake an investigative observation of the kinds of human beings who populate the institutions in which they conduct the business of human living, and more concretely, if we focus on the activities they perform to realize their life projects, we discover that the basic elements of these projects, which are revealed in what they do, are similar in kind to the elements that underlie the design of our individual life projects as particular subjectivities. They think, feel, make decisions, act, and pursue similar purposes to ours, as if we share the same nature, except that we realize the same nature differently, according to the different ways and environments in which we happen to exist. Regardless of who we are as individuals, the station of our lives, economic status, level of education, religious affiliation, or cultural orientation, do we not strive as human beings to build families, go to school, desire to eat and drink, need to rest once in a while, worship the Ultimate, enjoy social life, experience pleasure and pain, love, hate? In short, do we not see ourselves in others as human realities, and do they not see themselves in us as human realties? They do not only speak the natural language that declares their natural identity but also the language that declares their human identity. The point I am trying to accentuate is that even though subjectivity is the source and ontic locus of the human essence, that is, of that which makes us human realities, we know, interact, and treat each other as human beings by analogy. Others appear to us, act, react, and exist the way we do, even though we do not, and cannot, have cognitive access to the human essence that shines in their minds and hearts; we do not directly feel the human radiance of this essence.

But, my critic would now interject, can we not directly feel the radiance of the human other in certain religious, moral, intellectual, aesthetic, or romantic experiences? Do a man and a woman who are in love with each other not feel this radiance in the heat of a romantic union? Does the beneficiary of an act of compassion not feel the radiance of the human essence of the benefactor? Does a friend not feel the humanity of their friend? In the midst of a serious conversation, sharing important experiences, or cooperating on worthwhile projects? Do we not frequently feel the humanity of a stranger or of a lonely, joyful, or sad person? In these and similar life situations, does the radiance of the human essence not ooze out of the active presence of the human other?

I readily grant the possibility of feeling the humanity of the human other directly in different life situations or human encounters. I can add that having this feeling is one of the loftiest, most beautiful, most life-enhancing feelings we can experience in the tortuous course of our lives. I can further assert that the warmth and magical power of the human essence can penetrate the walls of the human body and transcend its boundary mainly because this power is one of its essential attributes. But this direct feeling is generically different from the direct cognitive act of its essential nature or the capacities that make up its structure. I can characterize this feeling as a kind of human presence in the fullness of its grandeur, as the greatest kind of reality in the world. It is quite possible that having this feeling is a necessary condition of the possibility of self-knowledge in the mode of inspecting subjectivity, as well as in the mode of knowing the human other. The actions, general behavior, or works of other human beings are embodiments of the essence that gives rise to them. We climb on their wings in our pursuit of the nature of their source. Moreover, we recognize, also by analogy, what they do in their immediate and mediate environment.

A Conception of Human Nature

If we classify the kinds of activities they perform, we discover that they are practical, aesthetic, religious, moral, intellectual, emotional, and individual. This classification warrants the inference of the presence of the faculty of intellect, affection, volition, and sensibility.

A significant advantage of identifying the humanity of the people in our social environment is that it provides a window in the wall of subjectivity of other human beings and allows us to glean not only the dynamics of human nature and what it achieves on the ground of reality but also what they *can* achieve, that is, its possibilities. No two human beings are alike in the extent to which they grow and develop as human individuals. Some are more skilled, endowed, and successful in the practice of the art of self-realization. Do we not learn much from observing or studying the lives of our family members, friends, neighbors, coworkers, teachers, and the multitude of social encounters in the areas of social life? Do we not learn how to be creative individuals by observing the people who are successful or distinguished as models of human living? The human as such is inspirational, motivational, and invigorating.

The third domain of human embodiment in which the human essence reveals itself concretely in the world is the sum total of humanity's achievements since the dawn of its birth and development millennia ago: human civilization. These achievements are human artifacts, but in this discourse, I treat them as human creations mainly because they are not emergent from the natural process and because they are the handiwork of the human essence in the spheres of human experience. When we study the history of human civilization, we stand before a vast and impressive array of creations. Historians classify them into general classes and types. They include what humankind did, created, believed, and valued and how people lived. However, we can also classify them in terms of their kinds: science, philosophy, art, technology, religion, mathematics, momentous events, cultural outlooks or orientations, and social institutions and organizations. We study or explore the nature of past civilizations, for example, Egyptian, Greek, or Chinese civilizations, by an examination of the creations, or artifacts, they left behind. They are usually preserved in libraries, museums, institutions, geographical sites, and the minds of scholars. They are human embodiments regardless of whether an artifact is a temple, a scientific treatise, a musical instrument, a painting, a building, a needle, a book, a cooking pot, or a weapon. Each one is a realization of a human design, purpose, or value. Although the human beings who created them do not exist, the human mind that created them lingers in them by virtue of the fact that their form, or design, embodies or expresses a manifestation of the human essence. An artifact is a telic object: its form declares, in the sense of revealing, its nature. Metaphorically speaking, I can say that the form of an object is the language the object speaks. Any type of human expression is a symbolic means of communication. We can extend the application of this principle to any type of natural or human formal organization. For example, we read the nature of an object, be it an entity, a natural scene, or an instrument, even the cosmos, by apprehending the significance implicit in its form. It is plausible to say that a scientific theory, a philosophical conception, or a system is an articulation of the meaning into a kind of formal organization. Accordingly, we know if an object is an artifact, that is, an object that embodies a manifestation of the human essence, because we know what it means for such an object to be a human reality, and we know what it means for something to be a human reality because we individually *qua* subjectivity know what it means for any phenomenon to be a human phenomenon.

We acquire knowledge of the human essence in any mode or instance of its manifestation in the domain of subjectivity, introspectively, and the living reality of the other human beings by observation. However, the extent of this knowledge is, to some degree, limited because it is individual. The capacity of the human being to explore the human mind in its structure and possibilities of creation and realization, or the laws that govern its creative powers, is insufficient, confined, and lacks the means of experiencing the inexhaustible depth of its being and the depth of the world around it. In contrast, the domain of human embodiments that constitute the history of human civilization represents the work of the individual and collective human mind not only in general but also in every sphere of human experience, for example, science, art, philosophy, religion, technology, and the areas of culture. Standing as an inquirer before this remarkable mosaic of human achievements is, in effect, standing before the works of the collective mind of humanity in the diversity of its achievements. In its omnipresence in the human community in the different parts of the world and in the different periods of historical development, the creative power of the human essence *qua* intellect, affection, and volition is revealed dramatically and more extensively than it can be revealed by the achievements of the human individual regardless of the greatness of their genius. It takes several lifetimes to be able to comprehend the nature and meaning of these achievements intellectually, aesthetically, religiously, technologically, morally, politically, and socially. This mode of standing is the basis of any kind of scientific, philosophical, theological, artistic, technological, and social inquiry. Do contemporary artists, scientists, philosophers, technologists, and social reformers not stand on the shoulders of past inquirers and on the periphery of the most recent findings in their areas of research?

Moreover, we assume this mode of standing in the cultivation of the minds of our rising youth. For example, the pillars of the curriculum of contemporary liberal arts institutions are the basic principles of the sciences and humanities. These and related academic disciplines are the basis of cultivating an enlightened and well-rounded human character. This type of character grows and develops from (1) a rich and versatile fund of human knowledge, feeling, imagination, and understanding, and (2) the necessary skill for making rational decisions in personal, social, and professional experience. I would not be amiss if I say that living from the wealth of the highest realizations of the human essence in the diversity of its manifestations is the foundation not only of human happiness but also of human destiny. I am quite aware of the fact that this assumption to an extent opposes, if not contradicts, the prevalent understanding, goals, and practices of education at the home and in the academy, which tends to conceive the aims of education as career, professional, or technical education, namely, preparing the young for a career in farming, engineering, construction, politics, law, medicine, teaching, business, or soldiering. The values that underlie this approach to education are survival, success, comfort, and pleasure. This educational issue is complex and contentious. It is not my intention to broach it in this context. I briefly referenced it only to emphasize that professional education should be a part of human education, which focuses on the education of human character. Professional competence should be (1) an ingredient and (2) a necessary condition for growing and developing as a well-rounded individual. A cultivated human character tends to make a good and successful professional; in contrast, a mediocre character tends to make a mediocre professional. Securing the basic conditions of survival is not enough; it is more important to survive as a fulfilled human being.

STRUCTURE OF THE HUMAN ESSENCE

The principal conceptual pillar on which the preceding conception of human nature stands is that the primary impulse in the human essence is human survival. As a thrust for being, the human essence does not aim to exist merely at biological survival but primarily at human survival, that is, survival of the human body as a human reality, as a reality whose life originates from the human impulse. In this context, any talk about human survival is a talk about human life because, unlike the animals that roam the wild and the plants that spring from the belly of the earth and live and die according to the laws of nature, human beings do not only thrive; they also flourish, that is, grow and develop from within. The possibilities of their existence are limitless. They do not act, at least not directly, according to the laws of nature but to the laws that spring from the human essence. The life of the human body thrives according to the laws of nature. This mode of survival is a necessary condition for human survival. The reason for the existence of the science of medicine and medical technology is to discover the natural laws that govern the life of the body in the different contexts of the natural process—heat, cold, temperature, pressure, gravity, earthquakes, diseases—and the necessary conditions of survival. Moreover, maximization of the means of biological survival is inherently conducive to a more effective consciousness and conditions of human survival mainly because the body is not only natural but also human. Its formal organization is designed to survive as a human body. Implicit in this fact is that it survives as a body insofar as it survives as a human body. Can I survive in the wild the way the lion or the fox survives if I am left alone? I can survive alone only if I develop the skill of acting and reacting to my natural environment the way the lion or the fox does.

As I pointed out earlier, human beings exist in nature but live in a human environment according to their wisdom. What is the nature of this environment? Any inquiry into the nature of human life should proceed from an adequate understanding of the structure of the human essence. What type of reality is it? What about it makes it a source of life that is uniquely different from the natural realm in which it is anchored? As a response to these questions, I can at once say that (1) this essence inheres in the formal organization of the human body as a potentiality and, more concretely, as a power, and (2) this power is a complex reality; as such, it is a dynamic structure. Let me elaborate on these two assertions.

First, the human essence derives its dynamism from the dynamic nature of the cosmic process from which it emerged. If we grant, as we should, that the essential nature of reality is process, we should *ipso facto* grant that the texture, or substance, of this process is power; accordingly, every kind

A Conception of Human Nature

of reality that emerges from it—physical, plant, and animal—should necessarily be essentially power. The assumption that logically and ontologically underpins this assertion, one that was conceived by Heraclitus and upheld in contemporary physics and metaphysics, is that change is inconceivable apart from the premise that an object cannot change if it is not *capable* of becoming different from itself in its present state from a state of being that precedes it, that is, if it does not have the *ability* to become different from what it is at the present moment. More concretely, if it does not have the "power to do" or "to become."[2] An ability is a drop, or quantum, of power. A human being who has the ability to design a house, negotiate a political or business transaction, teach, or farm a plot of land is one who has the capacity, or power, to design, negotiate, teach, or farm, that is, to do or produce something that did not exist before or change or modify the structure of an existing object. Any kind of change is not possible in the object of change if it is not capable of becoming different.

As a discrete reality, power does not exist as an object of sensual or intellectual conception; it inheres in the essential structure of physical or biological objects or entities. It is indispensable for the possibility of the existence of any kind of reality: to be is to be a reality, and to be a reality is to be capable of change. Power is the stuff of any type of reality. It does not exist in a niche or a corner, or as an element of a reality, but permeates and empowers every fiber of its constitution. As a reality, I do not merely have power; I am a complex drop of power. Indirectly, this insight lurks in Heraclitus's dictum that process (or change) is the essence of reality. The philosopher who articulated this dictum into one of the most elaborate, illuminating, and inspiring metaphysical conceptions of reality was Alfred N. Whitehead in his *Process and Reality*.

As a drop, and I can add as a flare, of power, the human essence is (1) a potentiality for realization or human growth and development, and (2) an inexhaustible possibility of realization in different forms and ways. This twofold feature warrants the assertion that it is a complex structure. But it cannot be a structure if it is not capable of being a source of different types of realization or modes of human experience, for example, social, moral, aesthetic, or religious experience. However, it is plausible to distinguish four types of capacities that constitute this structure: intellect, affection, volition, and sensibility. Each one of these capacities is a source of a primary type of experience: intellectual or rational, affective or appreciative, volitional or

---

2. *Webster's New World College Dictionary*.

desiring, sensory or acting. Implied in this categorization is that human nature manifests itself in and through these types of experience. Any inquiry into the substance of human nature, that is, the phenomenon that makes animal bipeds human realities, should, I submit, consider these domains of human experience as their field of inquiry, mainly because what human beings do or achieve in the world are emanations, or realizations, of these four structural elements of the human essence. The assumption that underlies this line of reasoning is that their concrete realization is their essence. They come to life in the experiences human beings undergo in the course of their daily lives. Alas! Do I exist outside the domain of these experiences? They derive their existence and human identity from the human essence.

Although I distinguish the structural capacities of the human essence as distinctive powers that generate distinctive types of human experience, they imply each other not only in terms of their mode of existence and how they function in the life of the human being but especially in terms of the kind of function they perform, mainly because they derive their being from the human essence as a unitary and distinct reality. First, if the primary impulse of the human essence is an impulse to human life, it would necessarily follow that their ultimate aim is to realize the impulse to human life; accordingly, they would inherently collaborate in the realization of this aim. It is, I think, reasonable to say that, as a propulsive power, they complement each other not only as parts of a whole but also as functions of this whole. This complementary relation reaches its highest point of integrity in the ability of the human being to undergo an experience of "I," "my," and "mine." It is difficult, if not impossible, to analyze or understand the nature of any capacity of human nature apart from an analysis or understanding the nature of the other three capacities, and it is equally difficult, if not impossible, for an activity of the intellect to know without including a measure of affection, volition, and sensibility, for the capacity of affection to appreciate the good and the bad or the beautiful and the ugly without an element of volition, cognition, an volition, and for the capacity of volition to make a decision without a measure of cognition, affection, and sensibility. These intimate relations among the four capacities are what led some of the major axiologists from Plato to the present to argue that the true is beautiful and good, and the good is true and beautiful. Can a true practical or theoretical judgment be ugly? Can an ugly idea or action be good? Can a bad choice be conducive to human happiness? In contrast, can a bad human being be spiritually or morally a happy or an authentic human being?

A Conception of Human Nature

Second, the inherent possibility of the human essence to be a complex structure of four basal capacities is the basis of the ability of the human being to perform four basic types of experience. They are neither blind nor fortuitous; on the contrary, they are *telic* in character. Their primary aim is to promote human survival. The attainment of this aim exists in the capacity as a demand, and as a demand, it assumes the identity *of peremptory desire*. In this capacity, the desire acts as the basis of the decisions the human being makes in the course of their theoretical and practical life This feature of the human essence sheds ample light on the generally recognized idea that (1) human beings by nature desire the true, the good, and the beautiful, and (2) meeting this desire is the basis of human self-realization, completion, or self-fulfillment. Let me illustrate the reasonableness of this claim in some detail.

First, "desire" comes from the Latin *desidere*, which means "to await from the stars," namely, *de*, "from," and *sidus*, "star."[3] Awaiting that which comes from the stars or the gods implies that the awaited or anticipated object is preeminently wanted, craved, vital, or necessary. This root meaning of desire is clearly recognized by *Webster's New World College Dictionary*: "to wish or long for, crave, or covet." The peremptoriness of the four primary desires that emerge as the means of the realization of human survival is intrinsic to the impulse of human life. They inhere in it; they are not secondary or supervenient to the impulse, and they inhere in it as an emanation from the human essence. This aspect of the peremptory desires is the ontic basis for saying that human beings by nature desire to know or seek the truth; appreciate the beautiful; value the good, the right, the holy; and to be free. Is it an accident that many philosophers and social reformers treat these values as inalienable rights?

Second, the peremptoriness of the desires that inhere as urges in the quest for self-realization is a demand in the impulse to human life. The ontic locus of this inherence is not the human body but the human essence. However, the imperativeness of the impulse to human survival, which includes the survival of the body, is not a natural event; the laws of nature do not govern it. It is a human event. As I shall explain in the next part of this chapter, it takes place in the medium of self-realization, according to the logic and laws that emanate from the human essence. The desire comes to life in the mind and heart of the human being consciously, thoughtfully, and freely. Human beings do not desire it simply because they feel a

---

3. *Webster's New World College Dictionary*.

biological itch for it but because its realization fulfills them. They know that they are the authors of the activity of self-realization, and they know what it means to undergo this kind of activity.

EMERGENCE OF HUMAN VALUES

The pursuit of self-realization brings out the telic character of peremptory desires: they are aim-oriented drives. The aim of the intellect's capacity is to know: knowledge of oneself and the nature of the cosmic process, as well as the power that creates and steers it. The aim of the capacity of affection is to feel and appreciate the qualities of natural objects, human objects, and human situations. The aim of the capacity of volition is to make the right or appropriate decisions in promoting our well-being individually and communally. The aim of the capacity of sensibility is to secure the material conditions of survival as autonomous human beings.

However, identifying the nature of these aims as objects that meet the peremptory desires and demands of survival is not enough. The question that stares us in the face is this: What kind of knowledge does the capacity of the intellect aim at? What kind of qualities of natural objects, human objects, and human situations does the capacity of affection aim at? What kind of desires occasion the most appropriate means of attaining freedom or individuality? What kind of skills are effective in acting in the practical domain of our lives? Put differently, under what cognitive, affective, volitional, and practical conditions do these capacities maximize the satisfaction of these primary desires? If we reflect on the nature and dynamics of these capacities as emanations from the human essence, as well as the desires they generate, we discover that they are the formal foundation of four principal kinds of human experience in the theoretical and practical spheres of life. Generally, people by nature desire to know, appreciate beauty, esteem the right and the good, and strive to be free. Pursuing these aims is the substance of their lives.

Next, if we cast a second inquisitive and penetrative look at the logic and dynamics of peremptory desires, we discover that they underlie a *sense of importance*. The objects they aim at are important primarily because their realization is the basis of human fulfillment, happiness, or perfection. We deem an object, a quality, or an experience important inasmuch as it is meaningful or significant, or as it matters to us as individuals and communities. The basis of importance is human perfection: that which is important is that which fosters human well-being. Importance is, in turn, the basis of value: an object or an aim is valuable inasmuch as it is important.

Our conception, or understanding, of the values we aim to realize in our lives as individuals and communities is based on the sense of importance, and the sense of importance is rooted in the essential structure of the peremptory desires and the existential conditions in which they can be realized in a given cultural and material environment, that is, from the values that emerge from the peremptory needs implicit in the impulse of human survival. We may posit four primary values as existential responses to these needs: truth, love, beauty, sound judgment, and autonomy. They are primary because they are the source of derivative values. For example, truth is the source of values such as sagacity, appropriateness, authenticity, propriety, or integrity; beauty is the source of values such as grandeur, sublimity, grace, loveliness, or elegance; goodness is the source of values such as justice, love, friendship, compassion, courage, or promise-keeping; and freedom is the source of values such individuality, progress, success, dignity, or prosperity.

ONTOLOGICAL STATUS OF HUMAN VALUES

Value exists in two ontic modes: first, as a potentiality in the essential structure of the human essence and then in the mode of possibility for emergence as an existential response to the peremptory needs for survival and, second, as schemas that exist in the human mind as a general design or plan of action. The question that underlies these two modes of existence is, How can I actualize the human potentiality that inheres in the formal organization of the human body as a human individual? What does it mean to grow as an individual? The means and conditions of this growth are latent in the potentiality. The point that deserves special emphasis here is that the logic that underlies the dynamics of these means and conditions of this essence is also latent in this essence. They are not natural because the human potentiality is generically different from the potential that inheres in the structure of natural objects. Yet, they are not inconsistent with the natural laws that govern the growth of the body as a natural reality because the structure of the human potentiality (1) emerges from the formal organization of the human body, (2) inheres in it as a potentiality, and (3) exists for the sake of the growth and development of the realization of the human essence, like the way apples trees exist to produce apples. The structure of the potentiality of the apple tree or that of the lion is given as a ready-made structure, and the laws of nature determine its realization, but that of the human essence is not given as a ready-made structure but as a structure to be realized under natural conditions. The first are peculiar to the human essence, and the second are existential. The first are human, and the second are empirical or natural. If I give a voice to the human essence as a potentiality in need of realization, I can ask it:

"As a potentiality, you crave to be real. What is needed for you to be realized into a concrete reality?"

Look into my structure as a complex of peremptory needs and intimations—to what they say and especially to the desires implicit in them. If you do, you will discover, having heard their intimations, that they peremptorily desire, that is, crave, the values you have articulated as primary and derivative values. That which makes a concrete human reality enables me to exist in the medium of value experience, namely, meaning. I crave meaning. My inmost craving is to come to life as a flare of human meaning. The mode of existence of this flare is the mode of existence of spirit. As spirit, I exist as a potentiality, and as spirit, I exist as an actuality. This is my destiny.

In the process of listening to the craving implicit in my peremptory needs, which constitute the fabric of my being, you will necessarily glean the identity of the values I crave. They exist to your eyes and ears as particular demands, that is, as particular types of identities. This type of gleaning is not intellectual but intuitive and comes into being in your mind as an apprehension of the good, the true, and the beautiful. In this process of intuition, you do not perceive me as an articulate, defined, or concrete reality. You intuit me as an indeterminate reality that can be articulated and defined, becoming a concrete reality. Remember: no matter its mode of existence, human meaning is never a concrete object but always exists in the medium of human experience as a flare of spirit or, more descriptively, as a flame of life.

This primary intuitive apprehension of the structure of the human essence is the source of our conception of human values in their mode of existence as a schema. In this mode, value exists in the mind as a general concept; as such, it is a possibility for inexhaustible realizations in different ways and forms.

A Conception of Human Nature

EMERGENCE OF VALUES AS SCHEMAS

Insofar as values inhere in the human essence as a response to peremptory needs, their mode of existence remains an indeterminate possibility for concretization. Their concrete determinations depend on the physical, cultural, and human level of development of a particular social environment, that is, on its natural, intellectual, religious, moral, artistic, scientific, technological, and philosophical resources. If values come into being as an existential response to peremptory needs, it would follow that articulating them into schemas should be based on (1) the degree of cultural development of the community and (2) their material and human resources. As a schema, a value functions as a general plan or design that can be used in the activity of decision-making individually and communally.

However, the material and human resources vary from one society to another and from one historical period to another. Accordingly, the meaning and method of realizing a schema in one society may be differently conceived and realized from the way it is conceived and realized in another. But despite this difference, they express the peremptory needs of human beings throughout the world because they share the same human essence. The system of schemas retains this identity regardless of the variance of human and natural conditions of human existence. It reveals its universality, and it also reveals its abundant resourcefulness, versatility, and brilliance.

If we assume an inquiring bent of mind on the multitude of human cultures in our examination of their past and present, the way anthropologists do, we discover an amazing mosaic of systems of value schemas. This mosaic not only represents the inexhaustible possible realizations of the values that disclose the inner depth of the human essence but also inspires the creative mind to penetrate its depth and explore it in different ways and forms. Do we not feel impressed, enlightened, and elevated when we immerse our minds in the lives of the cultures of the world, especially those that have adventured into the vast terrain of possible creations? Do we not wish to linger in the world of these adventures? How can it be otherwise, or different, if the stuff of our being is spirit? The spiritual human does not exist anywhere else because it is divine.

You have so far advanced an explanation of the emergence and ontological status of human values, first, in the mode of potentiality and second, in the mode of differentiation into derivative types of schemas, my critic would respond. But the question that piques my curiosity as a critic is their mode of existence as concrete types of experience in the world. If value is a reality, it should be a kind of object of perception or reflection. In what sense is such a value an object? You have already argued that the human essence is embodied in subjectivity, other living human beings, and the realm of human civilization. But as embodiments, they cannot be such objects, at least directly, because they are not given as sensual qualities of given objects but as a potentiality for realization under certain experiential conditions. How do values come to life in the natural process without being natural or sensual realities yet in the medium of this process? How can the human being *qua* human reality control, appropriate, or in some way interact with or influence the natural environment?

This is a fair question. The logic of my answer to it is implicit in the preceding account of the generation of the human essence and the values that emerge from it.

Let me at once submit that values assert themselves in the world as concrete realities, if not more real than the reality of natural objects then *as realized meaning* that comes to life in the medium of individual and collective experience. This type of reality does not exist in the mode of mere feeling, which is fleeting, but in the mode of living experience that endures in time as a human reality. However, it does not exist in the world as a discrete perceptual reality but as lived reality. Ontologically, its mode of existence in the world is the mode of embodiment: we encounter it as an embodied reality. The world of subjectivity, which is given to my mind in a moment of introspection as a psychological domain of existence, is transformed into a human world when I comprehend it in light of consciousness as my world, when I feel ownership of its ideas, emotions, images, moods, and experiences, dispositions, and the totality of the content that makes up its structure. Every element of this structure, which is an artifact or a creation of my mind, is an embodiment of an activity it has directly or indirectly performed. I feel the dimension of this psychological world inasmuch as I comprehend it as my creation, and I can comprehend it in this manner when I grasp its unity as emanating from my mind. For example, the idea that exists in some corner of my mind exists in that corner as a schema, that is, as a possibility for the recognition of a content of meaning. When I realize this content by an act of apprehension, the idea ceases to be a psychological entity and rises in the mind as a drop or flare of meaning. The "I" that presides over the domain of my subjectivity comes to life as a human reality in a reflective moment of introspection. When I act in the world as a conscious human being, I do not act as a biped; I act as a human biped; I act as a biped that embodies the human essence. I endure as a living human reality as long as my body endures.

By the same token, living human beings in my social environment are human embodiments. I cannot know or interact with them as human beings by my sensuous faculty, that is, merely by seeing, hearing, smelling, or touching them. They exist as automata to my senses, the way trees, rocks, lions, and rivers exist in nature. They surge—appear—as human realities in the medium of direct encounter or experience when I discern their humanity in and through the way they speak, look, or make a certain expressive gesture, or when I try to communicate with them in a conversation. In the course of ordinary social life, we take it for granted that the people who throng the alleys of social life are living human beings. We do this on the basis of past experience, habit, and faith generated by experience in general. We acquire the skill of distinguishing between a manikin or an automaton and real human beings by intuitive interpretation, especially when the social context in which we thrive is most of the time populated by living human beings. For example, in ordinary life, when a person acts strangely, abnormally, weirdly, irregularly, or unconventionally, do we not ask them "to be real"? Again, do we not characterize heartless and ruthless leaders or parents as inhuman when they harshly abuse other human beings? Do we not sometimes cry "be human!" or "you are not human!"? But the standard by which we determine whether a body is a human body is social convention and practice. Still, social conventions differ from one society to another and from one historical period to another. However, in ordinary life, the basis of treating those around us as living human beings is an intuitive interpretation based on experience.

Let us now cast a glance at the artifacts that comprise the realm of civilization. The human beings who made up the landscape of past civilizations, for example, ancient Egypt, China, Persia, India, Greece, or Rome, do not exist anymore. What exists are the remains they left behind, namely, different types of artifacts—buildings, clothes, knives, ships, cars, pictures, and similar artifacts. These are nonliving objects. Their given ontological status is similar to the status of natural objects. Artifacts are telic objects. They speak, and the language they speak is human. They speak it by means of their form. Unlike the form of a natural object, which declares the identity of the object, an artifact is a human formation. For example, we know what an object such as a knife is. Its form expresses a purpose or a value. If we discover in an archaeological dig of a past culture an object that looks like a knife, and if we know this particular kind of formation, or form, of this object, we can conclude that the culture being explored used knives. The discovered object looks like a knife and functions as a knife. Therefore, we can treat it as a human embodiment. The logic according to which we treat the knife as a human embodiment can be extended to the remains of past cultures. It is not an accident that we preserve the remains of past cultures in museums, libraries, certain landscapes, or gardens. They are the source of our knowledge of the achievements of past cultures and the creative possibilities of the human mind. The artificial dimension of the human world is not restricted to past cultures; it includes the contemporary, that is, living, worlds of the different societies of the world.

THE BUILT ENVIRONMENT

I can now advance the thesis, which appeared more than once in the preceding discussion, that human beings live in a built environment: they live in a human world. Although it is not natural, in the sense that its stuff is not physical or natural, it is anchored, that is, exists, in nature and is dependent for its existence on the dynamics of the natural process. It is the premium emergent of this process the way the aesthetic object that does not exist as a part of the physical constitution of the artwork is the emergent of the dynamic interrelatedness of the elements that make up the structure of the constitution of the artwork and especially the way in which the aesthetic object inheres in it as a potentiality. The aesthetic object is the handiwork of the creative activity of the imagination during the process of its creation. Unlike the animals that roam the wild and treat it as their home, human beings roam a human world they create and treat as their home. This thesis contains two constitutive propositions: (1) the human being is a value reality, and (2) the human world is also a value reality. It can use the resources of its natural environment but cannot exist in it as a natural reality. It may thrive in it as a body, but it cannot flourish in it as a human body.

THE HUMAN BEING AS A VALUE REALITY

The human being has a dual nature. The first is physical, and the sphere of its existence is the human body. The second is human or spiritual, and the sphere of its existence is the concrete manifestations that emanate from the human essence, which exists in the formal organization of the human body as a potentiality. The first is given as a natural object, and the second is given as a nonnatural object. The miracle, which reveals the inherence of a nonphysical reality in a physical reality, is one of the most recalcitrant aporias in the whole field of philosophy: How can that which is spiritual emerge from that which is physical? However, if we view the essential nature of reality in all its dimensions as a process, if this process is a creative advance—and it is, if this advance manifest itself in the emergence of myriads of types of classes of realities, physical, plants, and animals—we should, logically and ontologically, expect the possibility of the emergence of the human essence. But this is not merely a logical possibility; it is also an existential reality primarily because the emergence of the human essence inheres in the formal organization of the human body, which in contrast to any other emergent, is a novel emergent. The insight that underlies this line of reasoning, which did not seem palpable in the past, has received empirical support from contemporary neuroscience, according to whose findings the human dimension of the human being is centered in the brain as the primary organ of the human body. The active and interactive relation between the human subject and the functions of the brain lends credibility to the claim that the human essence inheres as a potentiality in the formal organization of the human body. There is no need for me to explain in detail this intricate relationship mainly because it is now clear that human activities or functions are causally interrelated, mainly because the human essence inheres in the formal organization of the human body. This interrelatedness does not necessarily imply that the human is reducible to the physical primarily because that which is human comes to life in the medium of human experience, which is a nonphysical reality.

A further aspect of the validity of this claim is that the "humanity" of the human being is not given as a ready-made reality but as a reality in process, that is, in a continual process of growth and development contrary to the classical view, according to which "humanity" is a metaphysical kind of reality. It comes into being as a subject that presides over the life of a human being at the peak of adolescence, when the growing youth welcomes the emergence of the capacity of self-consciousness. This moment signifies the emergence of the human essence as a discrete reality, that is, as a reality that can assume responsibility for its life. Prior to this moment, the youth exists and lives as a potential human being. Its emergence is concomitant with the development and maturation of the human body. The emergence of the human essence from the formal organization of the human body takes place when the body matures. In the meantime, the conditions of material and social life conspire to cultivate in the youth the necessary skills of acting as a human being.

What are the dynamics of this cultivation? Let us assume, as we should, that the substance of this cultivation consists of transforming the body of the youth, which is a particular lump of flesh, into a human lump of flesh. How does this transformation take place? How does this body act as a human reality even though its human dimension is not one of its parts? As a particular kind of organism, a body would not be a human body if it were not capable of being conditioned or trained to act according to the logic and aims of the possibility of the immanence of the human essence in its formal organization.

The process of cultivation begins when the child leaves the womb of its mother, in which its body is transformed into a human body. The substance of this process consists of the development of *human character*. The building blocks of this character, as Aristotle insightfully argued some time ago and has ever since become the fundamental principle of education, are dispositions, inclinations, or habits. They are instilled in the mind of the youth as elements constitutive of the character of the child. The instillation of these dispositions generates the psychological dimension of the mind. The principle of instilling them is the totality of the intellectual, moral, aesthetic, religious, social, and metaphysical values that underlie the possibility of growth and development of the life of the individual. As dispositions, they are the spring, or impetus, of the motives or drives of the desires and aspirations of human beings in general. They are the basis of saying that human beings are by nature rational, social, political, religious, or aesthetic. The instillation of these dispositions is possible because the values on which they are founded are existential emanations from the human essence as a potentiality. The human body is the receptacle in which these dispositions are instilled in the youth. It functions as a receptacle by virtue of the fact that (1) the human essence inheres in the body as a potentiality, which implies that it humanizes its inherence in every fiber of its being, and (2) its realization proceeds from the instillation, or ingression, of the values as dispositions. However, the instillation of human values not only explains but also justifies the thesis that the cultivation of human character and its development is the process in which the human essence inhabits the human body. This habitation transforms the body from being a natural object into a human reality.

A Conception of Human Nature

However, the body comes to life as a human reality only insofar as its actions emanate from the values in virtue of which it is a human being because, although the character is not a concrete being, it does not and cannot exist independently but in the midst of realized humanity. It comes to life as a reality, as a fact in the world, only when the potentiality exists in its active mode, that is, as a living reality. This assertion is corroborated by the fact that the child is not a human reality but a potential human being. We cease to be human realities when we go to sleep, or when we are comatose, or under the sway of a severe mental derangement. The human as such does not exist as a natural object but as a body that embodies the human essence, which shines in its true radiance in the medium of human experience. Outside this experience, it exists in the mode of potentiality. Accordingly, it is reasonable to say that the human body is a human embodiment. The structure of this embodiment, namely, human character, is a value reality because it rests on human values and its constitutive capacities are realized human values. But even though it inheres in the body, it exists in the world as a realized meaning. The human body oozes humanness the way a lion oozes lion-ness or the way an apple tree oozes apple-ness. Do we not actually live in the medium in the stream of experiences that come to life when we open our eyes in the morning and cease to exist when we sleep in the evening? What is the stuff of these experiences? A close examination of this kind of stuff will show that they are social, professional, religious, cultural, intellectual, aesthetic, and practical or personal in nature. Do we not try to maximize the depth of these experiences? Do we not feel alive when we undergo them? Do we not feel our reality and the reality of the world in and through them? Most, if not all, people lose the sense of life, the desire to respond to the challenges of daily life, and the passion to grow and develop in our individuality when the flare of meaning in our minds and hearts dies. In contrast, the more we expand the dimension of realized meaning in our lives, the more we grow in the passion of life and relish the nectar of the tree of human life.

We do not need to consult the records of social counsellors, psychologists, or psychiatrists to ascertain the countless cases of human beings who lose the desire for human life tend to commit suicide or feel abandoned by a cruel society in an indifferent natural environment. We come upon this phenomenon in the context of filial, professional, and social encounters. Human life is a supreme good. The good is attractive; accordingly, human life, once actuated by human values, is desirable. A life that emanates from these values is a life that expresses the highest aspirations of the human impulse to life. This kind of life is versatile, exuberant, and productive. It is the antithesis of a dull, unproductive, or mediocre life. In contrast to the productive life, its existence is plagued with the malignant virus of repetition, waiting, and quiet despair. One wonders whether a human being who leads such a life knows why they are living, why they will die, or what it means for them to come into being and pass out of being. This assertion stands erect on the assumption that the good, the true, the free, and the beautiful are not, as schemas that express the impulse to life, merely abstractions; they are flames of divine fire. The more the dimension of this fire expands in the life of the human being, the greater the tendency to pluck the fruits of joy and nobility from the original tree of life. The point that merits our attention in this context is that, regardless of who created the human race or why people exist in this world as sojourners, as guests at the banquet of the gods, it is a privilege to be invited to such a banquet. We are expected to enjoy every kind of culinary, aesthetic, intellectual, social, and religious experience. Could it be that the mystery of this invitation lies in the intention of the power that energizes the cosmic process and the event of the emergence of the human race?

It is not enough to argue that the human being is a value reality; it is equally important to argue that the environment in which they live is also a value environment. Can a reality that is nonphysical thrive and especially flourish in a physical environment? Obviously, the lion or apple tree can thrive in a physical environment, but can the human being thrive, much less flourish, in a physical environment? No. The human body is not designed the way the body of the lion or the apple tree is designed by virtue of their zoological and botanical bodies. They are sentient and responsive to their environment. This capacity reflects a measure of consciousness. But in addition to consciousness, the human body is capable of self-consciousness. This capacity reflects not only a different but also a higher kind of bodily formation. The human essence is an inherent aspect of this kind of formation. Soon after the animal is born, it can, by dint of instinct, adapt to its environment and thrive in it. But if it is left alone soon after the human body is born, it cannot survive as a human reality. The first expression, which it communicates by fits of crying and frantic bodily movements of its arms and legs, is a need for its mother's arms and breast, a clean groin, and the urge to be free. If these elemental needs are not provided, it dies. The mother and soon the father represent concretely the presence of the human environment, which is necessary for its continual growth and development. This process begins with learning how to walk, speak, eat, go to the bathroom, and play. Then, it slowly yet gradually acquires and develops social, intellectual, affectional, and volitional skills, all of which are necessary for its continual survival. But it cannot stop at the level of survival because another kind of need emerges in its consciousness permanently demanding fulfillment: the need to know, love, and be loved; to associate with other human beings; to appreciate beautiful things; to know the nature of its existence and the existence of this marvelous universe; and most of all to be a self-governed human being. Soon after these modes of consciousness bloom, it intuitively discovers that it is not merely different from its natural environment but that it is a human reality and that it acts from within, not as a body but as a special kind of power different from any other kind power, or force, in its natural environment. What is more startling is that it discovers that, unlike the apple tree that sits in its backyard and remains in its place until it dies, its existence consists of continually growing and developing. How? Why was it created? This consciousness creeps into its mind the way a cancerous cell creeps into an animal's body.

The purpose of the preceding brief, simplistic, and sketchy outline of the genesis of the need for human environment as an indispensable condition for human survival is to introduce, if not spotlight, the concept of "built environment " or "human environment." What are the building blocks of this environment? In what sense is it a human environment? How does the human being grow and flourish in it?

I shall begin my response to these questions with a historical remark. The emergence and gradual development of the human environment in the early periods of human civilization is a macroscopic reflection of the growth and development of the human being from their infancy to maturity. This development is conditioned by (1) the natural conditions of the environment in which it occurs and (2) the cultural and material level of growth or progress. For example, the extent, richness, and versatility of the human resources in ancient Indian, Greek, or Egyptian societies are rudimentary compared to those of the Middle Ages, and those of the Middle Ages are almost rudimentary compared to those in the contemporary period. The progress of human culture, in the widest sense of the word "culture," has been slow, gradual, and cumulative. But regardless of the level of its sophistication or perfection, the development of the human environment depends on the extent to which human beings are able to (1) grow in the dimensions of the capacities that make up the structure of the human essence and (2) appropriate the natural environment in meeting their rising peremptory demands. For example, the peremptory needs of people who lived in ancient Egypt are far less than those in the advanced societies of the contemporary world. The growth of these needs is always commensurate with human intellectual, aesthetic, religious, scientific, technological, political, and social growth and development.

Given the premise I have already defended, that the human being is a value reality, what is the structure, or the building blocks, of the environment in which they can flourish as a human being? This is not a rhetorical question. It stems from the present environment in which people flourish. Let us reflect on this environment in any part of the contemporary world. If we do, we discover that it is conducted in the medium of the institutions and organizations that make up the structure of society: family, government, school, workplace, religious establishment, art, science, philosophy, technology, army, and industrial centers. These and subsidiary social formations are the spheres in which contemporary human beings conduct their lives from the moment they are born to when they die. As I have indicated more than once, human beings exist in nature but thrive and flourish in a human environment.

The preceding premise is based on the fundamental, unshakable assumption that human values are the foundation of the institutions and organizations that make up the fabric of social existence. For example, the system of government based on values such as justice, freedom, security, and prosperity; the system of educations based on values such as truth, wisdom, human growth, individuality, and intellectual enlightenment; the religious establishment based on values such love, mercy, compassion, reverence for the Ultimate, and inner peace; the institutions of science, art, and philosophy based on values such as truth, understanding, beauty, and human progress; and the institution of technology based on values such comfort, survival, community, and human progress. In short, whether it is a settlement, village, city, megacity, or metropolis, it is one of transforming the natural environment into a human environment. Practically, the contemporary human being thrives in this kind of environment. For example, the child lives at home. In the morning, they go to school by bus; spend some time in the classroom, the playground, or the cafeteria; and then return home. They play in the backyard or their room. The ordinary adult follows the same pattern of activity in meeting the needs of their personal, family, professional, social, or religious life. Every place they stand, move, or perform a certain activity is a type of built environment. Each one of these places is designed as a medium in which people grow and develop as human beings. People create a human environment to create themselves and flourish as human beings.

However, the magnitude—depth, extent, or measure—of the human dimension of the built environment varies with the variance of society's material and spiritual resources. Although it is minimal in a nomadic or tribal way of life, it is maximal in the democratic way of life. The ability of the tribe to transform its environment into a built environment is limited. Its life is to a great extent dependent on the forces of nature and its limited capacity to meet the peremptory needs that are inherent in the human essence effectively or comprehensively. It took humankind several millennia to explore, discover, and realize the capacities that make up the structure of the human essence, and it will take more time to perfect their exploration and realization. The possibilities inherent in these capacities are inexhaustible.

Why do you say that the magnitude of the human dimension reaches its maximal degree of realization in the democratic way of life, my critic would suddenly interject. Is it not possible to envision a better or more desirable way of life? You seem to be certain about the superiority of the democratic way of life. What is the basis of this certainty? How can you justify it?

Unlike any other type of political constitution, written or unwritten, now and in the past, the ground on which the democratic constitution stands is the will of the people as a human community. This ground is generally articulated in a document or statement, usually called the preamble. The word "preamble" comes from the Latin *praeambulus*, "going before," which is in turn derived from *praeambulare*, "to precede"; *prae*, "before"; and *ambulare*, "to go."[4] The articles of the US Constitution are based on the dictates of the preamble; put differently, the articles are founded on it. The preamble is treated as an introduction to the Constitution. Ontologically, it is its source as a structural document. If I am to express myself analogically, I can say that the preamble is the root of a tree, the Constitution is the trunk, and the branches are a system of government. The government is a concrete objectification of the articles of the Constitution. The relation among these three elements is organic and not external, superimposed, or

---

4. *Webster's New World College Dictionary.*

supervenient. The basis of this organicity is the fact that, as a declaration of the will of the people, the preamble expresses the supreme values of the people as a human community. An examination of the preambles of the contemporary democratic constitutions will, I think, show that they are a set of human values such as freedom, dignity, justice, prosperity, happiness, solidarity, defense, peace, and equality.

Next, the constitution is an articulation of the values as an expression of their will. If I give the community a voice, this is what it will declare: the purpose of the constitution and consequently of the government that is founded in it is to create the public conditions under which we can live as a human community. These values are not only the basis of the sense that unites and transforms us into human community but also into a political community. But more importantly, these values are the foundation of our lives. Living according to their essential precepts is (1) the basis of a way of life and (2) the high road to self-fulfillment: freedom. That is, freedom is not merely a distant goal, and it is not merely a condition for living as a human community; it is a goal in progress. This goal is immanent in the process of realizing these values in our theoretical and practical lives. We desire to be a free people, and we exist as a free people inasmuch as our lives are shining examples of these values and their derivatives. We have no illusions about the meaning of human life. We know that the universe is not merely a process but an advancing, progressive process. Accordingly, we know that human life and the existential conditions in which we thrive are constantly changing and developing. If there is any moment or state of perfection, it consists of maximizing the greatest possible realization of the values that emanate from our inmost being in our living here and now. The democratic state is a human creation. It is not an ideal political state. This ideal exists as an ideal in process. Perfection is perfection of what we do in the present moment. It is always relative to the human and existential resources of the individual. The values we aspire to realize in our lives are no more than schemas that function as guideposts in the way we design and implement our life projects.

The democratic state is not a holy or sacrosanct system of government. It is an instrument we choose to create the material and human conditions under which we can live as a free people. It cannot be imposed on us; it should emanate from our collective will. No other society or authority can dictate how we should live because they cannot live our lives, and they cannot live our lives because their minds and hearts are not ours! The life of the human being and that of a society is neither repeatable nor replaceable.

Accordingly, imposing a way of life on other individuals or societies is tantamount to enslaving them. A slave exists as an instrument, not as a human reality. Living as a human individual, one who authors one's life, is an inalienable right, which implies the privilege to employ every possible means to protect it.

How do you justify possession of this right, my critic would abruptly intervene with a soft smile on their lips. What makes it warrantable, at least defensible? That smile would spring from the spirit of dialogue, of a desire to seek the truth of an essential aspect of human existence.

As an answer to this question, I can plausibly posit that the right to freedom, which consists of the privilege to self-government, or living as an autonomous being, originates from the fact that the human essence is not a gift granted by a metaphysical, natural, or human power but emerges as a peremptory demand from the human essence, which in turn emerges from the bosom of the cosmic process as one of its, if not the most, significant creations. As I have already argued in some detail, this essence exists in the formal organization of the human body as a potentiality and nowhere else. Its capacity of self-government is one of its inherent powers. Its existence is always individual. The impulse to human survival is rooted in the human body as a natural reality. Ontologically, it resists any kind of power that tends to govern the logic and process of realizing itself in the world. However, it cannot do this alone, that is, as a stick, but in the medium of a human community. Communal existence is a necessary condition for the possibility of individuality. Outside the sphere of human community, individuality and, consequently, freedom are a fiction.

Let me hasten to add that community and individuality are not opposites; they imply each other. The human being realizes their life as an individual in the medium of a community. Otherwise, its mode of existence would be the mode of an agglomeration. I emphasize this aspect of community as an essential feature of the democratic state mainly to spotlight the fact that the building blocks of the democratic state are human values, and the existence of the government as a concretization of the constitution is a structure of realized values. If I revisit Plato's idea that the state is the human soul writ large, I can say that the constitution of the democratic state is the preamble, that is, the will of the people, writ large. It is a translation of the conceptual structure of the constitution into a concrete, living reality. Its spirit, which emerges from the minds and hearts of the people, is the power that energizes the life and progress of the state as a human community.

CHAPTER THREE

The Need for an Art of Human Living

INTRODUCTION

The human being is the center from which everything human in the world emanates and becomes real in the different spheres of human existence. Its emanations exist in the world as human achievements, and the achievements exist as human artifacts. They come to life as human phenomena in the medium of human experience, and outside this experience, they exist as potentialities in the objects that embody them. For example, artwork is a physical object like a tree or a rock; it comes to life as an aesthetic object, one that embodies beauty, that is, as a human reality, in the medium of the aesthetic experience. The temple is a physical object; it comes to life as a sacred place when it functions as a place in which people revere God. The house is a physical object; it becomes a home, or a human dwelling, when it is used as a place for human living. This line of reasoning applies not only to the artifacts human beings create but also to the built environment in which people conduct the business of human living.

    The human world comes into being in and through the emergence of the human being from the human essence that exists as a potentiality in the formal organization of the human body. If you wipe out this center from the face of the earth, you also wipe out the human world in any of its manifestations. The human world begins to exist when the human being emerges from the womb of the human essence as a concrete reality. This assertion is based on the fundamental assumption that the human essence is an impulse, that is, an urge or thrust into existence or being. As an impulse, it is a drop of power; otherwise, it cannot be an urge or a thrust. This mode of existence is its nature and destiny in the world. It comes into being as a thrust and leaves the realm of being as a thrust. Do we not feel the intensity of this thrust when we perform our daily activities and especially when we feel the fingers of Master Time flirting with our necks?

A corollary to the claim that the human essence inheres as a potentiality in the formal organization of the human body is that the human being is not given to the world as a ready-made reality but as a reality to be made. Accordingly, because it is not made by nature or according to its laws, it must be a self-created reality. The capacity for self-creation is inherent in the human essence (1) as a power and (2) as a thrust for being in the world. The process of self-creation begins when the capacity of self-consciousness emerges at the peak of adolescence, when the growing person discovers, in a moment of miraculous development, that they are a "self," a "subject," or an actor—a being who is different from every other human or natural reality, that is, a being who can think, feel, and act on the basis of a personal capacity of thinking, feeling, and acting. It also discovers that, unlike another reality, it can design the project of its life and assume responsibility for its realization. What are the dynamics of this process?

The activity of self-creation is not a one-time event but an ongoing process. The emergence of self-consciousness is developmental in the sense that it is not completely *ex nihilo* but a transformational process in which the locus of the activity that comprises one's life shifts from one mode of being to a new mode and gradually assumes a new identity under the creative power, vision, and understanding of the new center of the self. This whole process is paradoxical for two reasons. First, every newly emerging moment of the self *is ex nihilo*. It signifies the coming into being of a new human reality for the first time. This event occurs in the womb of nature as a new human body emerges. It begins to exist as a potentiality at the moment of inception by virtue of its unique formal organization. The emergence of the human essence is concomitant with the emergence of the human body. As *bios* (life) is a novel emergence from the cosmic or natural process, the human essence emerges from the human species' body by its formal organization. This mode of organization is inherently capable of giving rise to the human essence or human nature. If, perchance, the body of the human being is impaired in a way that prevents it from acting as it should, or if the brain that oversees the functions of the body ceases to function according to its laws, the human body ceases to be a human body. This claim is grounded on the neuroscientific premise that the human essence—mind, human nature, reason, and spirit—emerges from the brain when the human organism comes to life after a period of sleep, during which the brain is not active at a conscious level. I say "conscious" because the brain is constantly active at the level of consciousness when we are awake and differently at the level of subconsciousness and unconsciousness when we are asleep. The emergence of the human essence is an unusual process. It is the result of a unique, unprecedented development in the cosmic process. The human brain is an occasion for such emergence because its neuronal structure is inherently capable of generating a special kind of *power field* that hovers around it. This field is the ontic locus of the human essence. Its complex structure emanates from different centers in the brain, each one of which performs a particular function. This is why if any one of these centers is damaged or weakened, the human being ceases to perform that particular function of the mind normally, and this is why it is possible to restore the human function of the mind if or when the function of the center in the brain is restored to its normal functioning.

Although the human essence comes into being as a potentiality and, as such, exists in the world as a novel emergent, it does not function as a self, subject, or individual until the capacity of self-consciousness emerges at the peak of adolescence. Self-consciousness is the birthplace of the human self or mind. It is a necessary condition for transforming the human body into human reality. The human being assumes the ontic status of "human individual" when it is conscious not merely of its biological needs and the world around it but also of itself as an independent reality, that is, as a center of being that thinks, feels, wills, and acts from within—put differently when it discovers that it is not only an independent reality but a reality that can weave the fabric of its life and destiny. Self-consciousness is a moment in which the growing person suddenly, as though by a strike of magical power, succeeds in standing before itself the way it stands before a mirror as a particular identity. In this self-encounter, it does not only recognize that it is the object of its consciousness but also its subject. It discovers that it is the subject and the object at the same time. The self that examines itself as an object sees itself as the subject of its being. This process of examination and discovery is not an event that takes place accidentally or fortuitously but an ongoing process of gradual growth, and it does not take place abstractly or objectively the way a biologist examines a cell or a rat but concretely in the medium of acting as a living. The self emerges in the light of its being as an object of reflection in a moment of serious intellectual, affectional, and concrete activities. Do we not see and feel ourselves as subjectivities and as depths of experience in moments of sickness, triumph, failure, or loss? Do we not discover our strengths, weaknesses, possibilities, true desires, or capabilities in such moments? Do some parents not encourage their children to undergo adventures in the spheres of life? Again, is travel not an effective means of enlightenment, education, and self-understanding?

As a basis of learning, understanding, and developing, self-consciousness is (1) an individual and (2) a collective or communal undertaking or endeavor because the growth and development of human society are essentially accumulative in terms of knowledge, experience, and creation. Like the individual who can, in moments of self-consciousness, stand before itself and reflect on the landscape of its capacities, possibilities, and achievement, a community can do the same. We think individually, but also we think collectively. Does the scientist, philosopher, social reformer, artist, and theologian not think, act, and create on the basis of the achievements of the inquirers that preceded them? Is this kind of thinking, acting, and creating not cooperative and communal? Does a society not live—see, act, and evaluate—from the standpoint of its past and vision of its future on the basis of its past? Can an agglomeration of human beings organize themselves into a conglomeration if their organization is not born in a state of collective self-consciousness? Does the preamble of the democracies of contemporary states not begin with "we the people"? Does this kind of declaration not arise from a community of mind and will? I focus attention on the phenomenon of self-consciousness as a necessary condition for the existence and flourishing of human life individually and communally.

The proposition that the human dimension of the human being exists as a potentiality in the formal organization of the human body logically and ontologically entails three basic assumptions that reflect three essential aspects of human existence. I submit that these aspects warrant the thesis that leading a human way of life, or a life worth living, is an art. The remainder of this chapter will be devoted to an elucidation and corroboration of these three aspects of human existence. In the following chapters, I shall discuss the sense in which human living is an art and the conditions under which this art is possible.

FIRST, THE HUMAN ESSENCE AS A POTENTIALITY

As I argued a moment ago, unlike trees, rocks, or lions, the human being does not exist in the world as a ready-made reality but as a reality to be made and, more concretely, to be created. I cannot be or live the being and life of another human being, although I can assume responsibility for the well-being of other people. I am responsible for the design as well as the implementation of my life project. My life consists of the process of its implementation, which revolves around the question of how I should live, love, and die. Accordingly, what are the principles and conditions of the realization of my life project? One can correctly say that I should be the source of the values and beliefs according to which I envision my life project and that these values and beliefs should be based on the peremptory desires that arise as an external response to the peremptory needs that are inherent in the structure of the human essence. If the life I should live is mine, it should meet the needs, urges, or appetites that exist as possibilities in the essential structure of my essence as a human reality. Otherwise, it would be difficult to say that the life I live is, in principle, truly mine or authentic. For instance, although the life I led before I became conscious of myself as an independent reality with a particular subjectivity, and although I was unable to undergo the genuine experience of "I," "mine," or "me," it was not, strictly speaking, mine, mainly because it was instilled in me by my immediate and mediate environment, of which I am an integral part. During this period, my mind was, practically speaking, a *social construct*. The beliefs and values on which I acted were not consciously, rationally, and willingly conceived, approved, or espoused by my mind and heart. Indeed, prior to the emergence of the capacity of self-consciousness, my "self" was an extension of the social self. Society thought, felt, and acted in and through my mind and heart. The problem is that I was not the author of the beliefs and values on which I acted. Of course, I thought them, I felt them, and I acted according to them, but I did this as an extension of the mind and heart of my social environment. The task of education in the major institutions in which we live is to train the young in how to think, feel, and act from within. Do we not, in the areas of practical life, frown upon or distance ourselves from people who are conformists, inauthentic, or superficial human beings in the intellectual, aesthetic, religious, and political areas of association or communication?

Now, under what existential conditions can a human being act and live from within, that is, from the reality that is the source of their humanity?

The Need for an Art of Human Living

How does the growing person, even the adult, discover, conceive, or acquire the basic beliefs and values that function as the basis of constructing the design of their life project or way of life? In what sense does the life of a genuine human being emanate from their mind and heart? I am quite aware of the fact that many people throughout the world, now and in the past, do not live on the basis of a clear and adequate self-understanding or on the basis of principles founded on the essential needs and demands of the human essence. On the contrary, if I take my critical observation, as well as the observation of the majority of existentialist philosophers, artists, and social reformers on the underpinnings of the lives of the majority of human beings in society, I can say that their lives are, to a great extent, imitations, quotations, or plagiarisms. This way of living is, to my mind, a clear case of "human waste." Regardless of the extent to which this situation is serious, widespread, or endemic, the question that merits critical analysis and appears as an unstoppable demand of our humanity is: How can I, as a human being, live authentically, that is, true to the demands of the human essence? Does the lion or the tree not strive to live according to the demands of its nature? Does the sun, the river, or the wind not act according to its nature? By the same token, should the human being not exist and live according to its nature? The nature of the lion, the tree, the sun, or the wind is given, but the nature of the human being, *qua* human reality, is not given as a ready-made reality. As I have argued, it does not exist as an object in the world but as a potentiality inherent in the formal organization of the human body, and it emerges into the light of day under certain developmental conditions. What is the nature of this potentiality? An adequate answer to this question, which will figure prominently in the second part of this chapter, is a necessary condition for understanding human nature.

In what sense does the human essence inhere in the human body? What type of reality is this potentiality? First, it does not inhere in the body as a quality or ingredient; otherwise, it would exist as an object that can be observed and studied by scientists. Second, it does not inhere in it as a ready-made reality the way the oak tree inheres in the acorn as a kind of structured object that comes into being under natural conditions. I suggest that it inheres in the body as a power and emerges from its formal organization as a flare of power. More concretely, it inheres in the *dynamic interrelatedness* of the elements that constitute the unique formal organization of the body. The human essence is a flare of power that inheres in *the way* the body is formed, the way the aesthetic object emerges from the formal organization of the elements that constitute the structure of the artwork as a representation. It is difficult to say that a potentiality, that is, a quantum of power, inheres in a passive medium or object. Otherwise, it would be tantamount to saying that it comes into being *ex nihilo* as a structured reality, which is impossible.

The human body is a particular and, I would add, unique organization. It emerges from the cosmic process as a novel reality under certain conditions of evolutionary development. The essential nature of the reality from it emerges as a process: change. However, the reality of change is not possible if the objects that change are not *capable* of change, that is, of becoming different from what they are at the moment of their existence. Again, discourse about any kind of capability is, in fact, discourse about "power." The elements, simple or complex, that constitute the structure of the cosmic process in the diversity of its dimensions are "provisional events": processes. The relations that exist among them are dynamic. There are no rests or stops, nor is there endurance, in the cosmic process. The only thing that endures is the continuity of change. This claim is corroborated not only by the Heraclitean metaphysical intuition that reality is process but also by the most recent findings of physics. Accordingly, the physical and biological dimensions of the human body are dynamic. This is why the phenomenon of life is inconceivable if the elements from which they emerge are not dynamic.

Every organism is a whole, and every whole is composed of parts. The whole is a unity of its parts. The aspect of unity is dynamic because the whole is constituted as an emergent by virtue of the dynamic interrelatedness of the parts that make up the structure of the whole. Moreover, the interrelatedness of the parts that make up the unity of the object and distinguish it from any other object can also be the basis of the emergence of other types of qualities or aspects. For example, mixing different types of elements in the field of chemistry with other elements that produce new objects or qualities is not possible if the elements are not capable of becoming or changing and consequently interacting with each other under certain conditions. The technologist in the different areas of practical and theoretical life is an expert in the dynamics and ways of mixing particular kinds of elements with each other.

Now, if we turn our attention to the human body, we encounter a unique type of whole. It is a composite of organs that exist in the body as a whole and as parts of a larger whole. The larger whole is a unity of the dynamic interrelatedness of the organs that make up the structure of the whole body. The human body is organized in a way that creates the conditions for the emergence of the human essence as a potentiality that inheres in the formal organization of its organs. As I emphasized earlier, this potentiality does not exist in this or that organ of the body but in the way they are organized and, more concretely, in their dynamic interrelatedness. It cannot emerge as a ready-made reality but as power. It originates from the bosom of the dynamic interrelation of the organs that are essentially processes after all!

What kind of power emerges from the formal organization of the human body? Unlike objects that emerge in the physical and biological domains of reality as ready-made realities, in the sense that their structure is given in the potentiality from which they emerge, the human essence emerges as an *indeterminate structure*, one that can be realized in different ways and forms. The concept of "indeterminate structure" may seem paradoxical, if not contradictory, because the concept of structure signifies an existing, established, or determinate form, but a critical reflection on the logic of creation will show that it is possible for an emergent structure to be composed of parts that are possibilities for becoming, or for being, transformed or realized in different ways and forms. Broadly, a structure is a kind of manner, arrangement, or organization of parts. The idea of part implies the idea of whole. It is inconceivable for one to exist without the other. In ordinary life, we experience the world around us according to the principle of Euclidean geometry, which assumes that reality is spatially stable, fixed, or given. But in contemporary physics and some philosophical systems such as Bergson's or Whitehead's, we experience the world dynamically, that is, as a process in a constant state of change or development. The assumption that underlies this kind of experience is that every element of reality is dynamic.

At this point in my analysis, I should emphasize that the structure of any emergent, regardless of whether it is human or natural, reflects the nature of the reality from which it emerges: its formal organization is inherent as a possibility in the womb that gives rise to it. Accordingly, if we grant, and we should, that the human body is a dynamic reality and, consequently, a complex kind of power, it should follow that, as an emergent, the human essence as a kind of power should inhere in the formal organization of the body as a complex power. This conclusion is warranted by the assumption, which I already discussed, that the human essence inheres in the totality of the form of the organization and not simply in this or that part of it.

We should now ask: What are the constitutive elements of the structure of the human essence? By what method can we discover or identify them? An effective, productive method is crucially important because a conception of the human essence directly or indirectly, implicitly or explicitly, negatively or positively, vaguely or clearly, functions as the basis of (1) self-understanding, individually and collectively, and (2) the articulation of the principles according to which we design and pursue our life projects. The method I employ in this discourse is phenomenological. Its principle was first expressed by Plato's dictum *that society is the individual (soul) writ large.* He assumed that society reflects the essential structure of the human soul or, put differently, the essential structure of society is a macroscopic manifestation of the structure of the soul. Next, if we grant that the nature of any object, human or natural, is comprehended by what it does or by the role it plays in its environment, then we can say that we can identify the nature of the constitutive elements of the human essence by an understanding of the kind of practical and theoretical activities human beings perform at the individual and communal levels of their existence. These types of activities—in science, philosophy, theology, religion, art, morals, and the ways of being in the world—are what human beings do. I can add to Plato's insight corollary dictum: the realm of civilization, which reveals itself in the achievements of human beings in the course of human history, is human nature writ large because it is the largest domain of what human beings do, have done, and can do.

This domain of inquiry into the nature of the human essence can be supplemented, and to some extent confirmed, by introspection, that is, by an examination of the domain of human subjectivity. In addition to philosophers, social scientists are skilled in conducting this kind of self-examination. Self-examination makes me tick as a human being? What are the vital powers, drives, or urges that make me strive to survive as a human being or to realize my life project? Or, expressed in simpler terms, what do I want as a human being? If I were to undertake this kind of examination, I would discover that I desire to know myself, nature, and the Ultimate, which is the task of the faculty of the intellect; to appreciate beauty and associate with other human beings individually and socially, which is the task of the faculty of affection; and to realize myself as a human individual, which is the task of the faculty of volition.

The Need for an Art of Human Living

Accordingly, in our attempt to explore the nature of the constitutive elements of the structure of the human essence, we should examine the kind of primary, generic, or distinctive activities human beings perform in the different spheres of their lives. This method is applied in the areas of science, philosophy, and theology. If I follow in the footsteps of taxonomical practice in the various fields of inquiry, and I do, I can say that the essential structure of the human essence consists of three main elements: thinking or intellect, affection or feeling, and willing or volition. Every type of activity human beings perform in their daily lives stems from one or more of these elements. It may seem strange that these elements are also constitutive elements of human action: purpose or rational vision, desire or passion, and will or volition—purpose, means of achieving it, and will to achieve it. They are, moreover, indispensable for both biological and human survival. I would not be amiss if I said that the impulse that underlies the emergence of human essence in the long, laborious, and innovative course of the cosmic process is an expression of the impulse for being—for life in its highest form.

The constitutive elements of the human essence exist as active agents of the human essence insofar as it inheres in the formal organization of the human body. They come to life as distinctive faculties when the power of self-consciousness emerges at the peak of adolescence. Although they represent different functions and act as if they are distinct or independent of each other, nevertheless, they emanate from the same essence as an impulse to human life. They conspire to make its realization possible. They do not only imply but also complement each other. Why? They are concrete expressions of the human essence as an impulse to life. I can express the same point by saying that the impulse to human life becomes concrete in the activities of these three faculties.

In the initial state of their mode of existence as constitutive elements of the impulse to life, they exist as drives or *peremptory* desires. I have emphasized "peremptory" because they are impulsive and compulsive in character. But as potentialities, their mode of existence is abstract because they are empty—empty of concrete beings. This emptiness creates a feeling of need. "Need" signifies lack or absence: we desire what we need. The three faculties I have identified as constitutive of the structure of the human essence are designed to be instruments of meeting the needs of human survival. Like desires, needs are peremptory because they arise as demands of the human essence; they inhere in it as an impulse. The peremptory desires arise as an existential response to the needs.

The next question that necessarily arises is, what are these needs? As I indicated earlier, these needs are knowledge, love, beauty, religiosity, and freedom. The object of the first is nature and human nature; of the second, other human beings, socially and communally; of the third, art and nature; of the fourth, God or the Ultimate; and of the fifth, the human being as an individual. I need to know the nature of the world around me, the society in which I live, human achievements, and myself. These three types of knowledge are requisites for meeting the conditions of the realization of the human essence, that is, for human growth and development. How can these conditions be met? I raise this question for two reasons: first, because this knowledge is relative and, second, because it is never perfect.

First, the knowledge on which human beings act is different from one region of the world to another and from one historical period to another. Although the knowledge of the scientist, philosopher, theologian, and social reformer is more reliable than that of the layperson, its dissemination or translation into practical principles of action is not easy, not only because it is hard to uproot established patterns of behavior or beliefs and values but also because the translation of theoretical knowledge into ways of living is inherently hard. For example, although the world of scientific, philosophical, and social reform is, in principle, available individually and communally, people on the ground of reality do not conduct their lives according to the truth propounded by the achievements of these areas of knowledge. Why? Second, the world of human knowledge is in a constant state of perfection. The universe is an infinite depth of being, and so is the world of the human mind. The history of ideas is a history of rising and falling theories, concepts, and views of the nature of physical and natural reality. People are always confronted with the formidable challenge of transforming this knowledge into viable ways of life.

This domain of inquiry into the structure of the human essence can be supplemented and, to some extent, confirmed by introspection, that is, by an examination of the domain of subjectivity. In addition to the philosopher, the social scientist is skilled in conducting this kind of examination. What is the secret that unlocks not only my existence but the way I should live, love, and die? What are the vital powers, drives, or urges that move me in my endeavor to lead a human way of living? If I were to undertake this kind of examination, I would discover that I desire to know, which is the task of the intellectual faculty; to associate with other human beings individually and socially, which is the task of the affectional faculty; and the desire to be, which is the task of the willing faculty.

However, it is not enough to argue that the thrust of the human essence is a thrust for being in the world and that this thrust generates peremptory desires that emerge as existential responses to peremptory needs inherent in the structure of human essence. It is equally important to know or formulate valid or reliable principles for meeting these desires. I should possess the right kind of knowledge or the right principles of action. The need to associate with others is not enough; I should associate with them under the conditions of respect for the beautiful, the good, the true, religiosity, and respect for human beings individually and collectively. In the endeavor to meet the necessary and sufficient conditions for leading a human way of life, it is, I think, plausible to propose that the intellect should aim at the value of truth; the faculty of affection at the values of goodness, beauty, and religiosity; and the faculty of volition at the value of freedom. These five values are primary because they directly reflect the essential demands of the preemptory needs. They are general and exist in the mind as *schemas*. As such, they do not apply to particular experiences directly but generally. As *schemas*, they signify the possibilities for realization in different ways and forms. Moreover, as primary, they have the potential for derivative values that can be applied to different kinds of experiences individually and collectively. For example, the value of truth is a possible source of values such as soundness, wisdom, fidelity, prudence, sagacity, or integrity; the value of the good is a possible source of values such as justice, friendship, honesty, courage, or compassion; the value of beauty is a possible source of values such as grace, grandeur, loveliness, tragedy, elegance, or enigma; the value of religiosity is a possible source of values such as humility, piety, faith, mercy, or love; and the value of freedom is a source of values such individuality, success, progress, prosperity, and peace.

I have made the preceding excursion into the ontological status of the human essence and the peremptory needs that arise from its essential structure mainly to spotlight the central question of this book: How should I live, love, and die as a human being? It necessarily springs either theoretically or existentially from the effort in which people try to meet the demands of human living. The crux of my argument is that if the human being is given to the world as a potentiality, the question that necessarily glares us in the face is, How should I realize this potentiality according to the logic and inner demands of the essence inherent in my essence?

SECOND, FINITUDE

The fundamental assumption that underlies this discourse and resists theoretical or practical doubt is that in all its forms, reality is a process. The universe and every element in it come into being at a certain point in time and pass out of being at a later time. The existence of the human being is not only temporal but also bounded by two moments—the moment of its birth and the moment of its death. This boundedness defines its finitude. But it is finite in a deeper sense of "finitude." It is an emergent; as such, it is a creature. The capacities that make up its structure as a particular nature are confined, or limited, to these capacities, which are given. These capacities constitute the structural dimension of its existence, reflection, and life. It cannot be other than what it is. Moreover, as a potentiality awaiting realization, it is limited by its given human resources. The discovery and means of realizing its capacities are dependent on its natural and human environment, which is always changing. Accordingly, if human life is thrust into the future, if the future is in principle unpredictable, at least not completely, or accurately, it should follow that the capacity of the human being to thrive as a human individual is limited by contingent, unpredictable, or random factors and possibilities.

The distinctive aspect of human finitude is not merely its boundedness between the events of birth and death, or the fact that it is a creature, but especially by the fact that it will pass away: death. It is strange how the majority of people celebrate the moment of birth and do their utmost to cover up the moment of death as if it were their worst enemy. Ironically, they rejoice at the moment of birth and tremble with fear and trepidation when death appears at the last horizon of their lives. The language of death, or its signification, is the language of its finitude. One experiences their finitude when they see, recognize, or existentially confront the slow approach to death. Life is good, an absolute good. The good should linger, and it should linger forever. Why should I die? This question arises regardless of whether one loves life or hates it. Alas, why should I be invited to the rite of human living? Yes, why should this creature—me, the writer of these words—be created out of the belly of nonbeing, conducted to the banquet of human living, and then with the wand of a malignant power, vanish from the realm of being?

I did not choose my existence. No one asked me whether I wanted to be created. Was my creation a freaky accident or perhaps a mistake or a joke? Does a nonbeing speak or choose the creation of this or that creature? Strangely, I discover that I, as a human subject, exist, and I discover this miraculous happening at the moment of the emergence of my self-consciousness at the peak of my adolescence. The reality I discover is neither concrete nor ready-made but a reality to be made. I also discovered that my life is a task: I am created as a task, as a possible life project. Am I supposed to be a Jupiter, a god that probes the depth of nonbeing and squeezes out of its heart and mind my existence and the existence of my fellow humans? Goodness! How can the potentiality that I am, which is an inexhaustible possibility of realization, create my life according to the demands of the essence that makes me a human reality? When I discover that I am a potentiality, I also discover that I have no choice merely to live but to chart the course of life according to the logic and given resources of my essence. Whether I become aware of the overpowering impact of this fact intuitively, or as an evolving consciousness along the way, I endeavor to assert my existence as a human individual. In my pursuit of this most important aim of my life, I begin, like a divine sculptor, carving the outline of my character into a living flare of human life. The more I proceed in the process of its creation, the more I discover that it is not easy but, on the contrary, intimidating, challenging, and sometimes crushing, oppressive, and vain. Nevertheless, the impulse to human life that pulsates in every fiber of my being gives me the needed hope, patience, courage, and passion to go on living with gusto. I taste the thrill of creation in the midst of pain, I frown upon the challenges of everyday living with a sense of triumph, and I pluck the fruit of my labor with a smile of ecstasy. During this process, I build a family, raise children, and give them the gift of life and the means to contribute to the well-being of society. I excel in my professional work and do all I can to be a responsible citizen. On more than one occasion in my daily existence, I take a break from my daily labor; I sit on the top of a hill outside and contemplate the amazing beauty and grandeur of nature and the miraculous and magnificent achievements of humanity in the various areas of human experience. A smile gently slides onto my lips! This smile is accompanied by a whisper: if there is a heaven, or a garden of Eden, it must be here in this world—in this evolving spectacle of nature and in the heaven of the human mind.

Suppose, my dear reader, you sit on top of this hill; suppose you contemplate this heaven; suppose you delight in savoring it with your intellectual, affectional, and volitional sensibilities; and suppose you marvel at its power and mystery—would you not wish to remain seated on top of that hill forever? Would you not wish to sizzle in the warmth of its love?

"Oh—love?" you wonder.

"Yes!" I say. And I say that it is the noblest, loftiest, and greatest kind of love. How can it be otherwise if it is not the most valuable act of divine giving and receiving the human heart and mind craves in this world? But neither I nor you can linger forever on top of that hill. Although reluctantly, we have to descend and flow with the current of the cosmic process, and we have to submit to the fact that our visit is *temporary*. I have emphasized "temporary" because Father Time, the hand in whose womb we received and were able to see the light being, gently strokes our shoulders as if to remind us that it is time for us to leave this world and return to the belly of nonbeing. The consciousness of this reminder is a request for preparation. But who in their right mind would desire to leave the rite of human living? Do I not shudder when I existentially stand at the rim of his consciousness, contemplate the marvel of the cosmic process, and nod my head with a feeling of sorrow about the inescapable destiny?

After that visit to the top of that hill, I stand before the mirror of truth, which Father Time left at the dressing of my living room, and reflect on the meaning of my existence: Why is my life short? Why should it end? Why was I created to these parents, this society, this corner of nature, and this historical period? Why was I nourished by the milk of this culture and not some other culture? More importantly, I wonder: Why was I not informed by some divine, or even evil, voice that all the struggles, all the pain, and all my achievements, which were and remain dear to my heart, will soon be buried in the graveyard of nonbeing? This question irks me sharply because it comes with the knowledge that, had I known that nonbeing is the co-master of all existence, I could have led a better way of life. I could have corrected many of my mistakes, fumbles, and blunders that tortured me more frequently than I could bear, and I could have prepared myself psychologically and spiritually before taking a last look at the marvelous spectacle of the cosmic process.

The Need for an Art of Human Living

I can think and comprehend the existence of every object or possible reality that exists or may exist, and I can observe the way other people die, but I can neither think nor comprehend my death. I cannot experience my nonbeing. I can experience my absence from this or that place but not from the universe! It may be too late, and frequently it is, to raise the question of self-validation when I stand at the edge of my existence: Can I justify the life I have so far lived? Was it worth living? I do not know whether the cosmic process bestows gifts, but from my point of view, my life is a gift. Do I deserve the gift of life that was granted to me? What if a devil who has been following this stream of reflections, or reverie, whispers that my life, and the life of every human being, is a negligible ripple in the cosmic process, that my existence and the existence of every part of the cosmic process is a necessary means to the realization of an infinitely valuable aim, and that my life and the life is destined to the wastebasket of the cosmic process?

But, regardless of whether the devil is right, and regardless of whether a beneficial power, one that speaks the language of the human soul, elevates me to a more refined kind of human life, the consciousness of death, whether I arrive at it intuitively or by observing the death of other people or by reading scientists' and philosophers' books, provokes the all-important question: How should I die, or with what spiritual frame of mind and heart should I approach the point of no return? Concern about or the fear of death, in the sense of the expiration of life from the body, is not the problem, for the event of expiration is not painful. The concern or fear stems from the fact that I do not wish, approve, or accept the cessation of my life because my life is dear to me, and I inherently cling to it and desire it forever. Although I cannot answer the question of the why of death with any measure of certainty, I can say with a measure of certainty that I can conceive the design of my *life project with the consciousness that I shall die.* This consciousness will prompt me and, I can add, encourage myself to conceive this design according to the values that emanate from my essence as a human being and do my best to live according to them with a deep sense of satisfaction and inner peace, no matter the hardships I may face in the process of realizing them.

I tend to think that a life well lived is a life that does not fear the advent of death. Why should I complain, feel depressed, or revolt against the world or the power that moves it at the realization that I, like everything that exists, will cease to exist? Consciousness of death need not, and should not, be omnipresent in every waking moment or every decision we make in the course of our daily lives. This kind of consciousness is both obstructive and destructive. A psychologist would characterize it as pathological. The design of one's life project and the way one implements it should be based on the consciousness that human life is temporal. This kind of consciousness obviates the possibility of being surprised when the moment to leave the world arrives. What matters is that living from within is the essence of fulfilling our destiny. Should we expect more?

THIRD, SOLITARINESS

A corollary to the fact that the life of the human being is finite or temporary is solitariness. The human essence from which human life emanates as a concrete reality inheres in the formal organization of the human body, which exists in the scheme of nature as a single, unitary, and independent reality; it is mutually exclusive of the existence of any other type of reality. My life originates from this particular reality. My body and the social environment around me are the means—materiel—of its realization. This exclusiveness is physical, psychological, and spiritual. The "I" that acts as a subject in the world is a world—a human world. The ontological landscape of this world is my subjectivity. It is windowless; no one can take a peek into it, much less enter it. I reveal some of its contents by conversation, confession, or inferentially by the way I act or express myself, or by the objects I produce. Implied in this feature of human existence is the fact that no one can live the life of another human being: human life is not transferrable. Transferable design and method of realization are a personal responsibility. I may receive ideas, counsel, advice, or a certain kind of enlightenment on how I should act or live from others, but the kind of life I live is always "mine" or "my" exclusive responsibility.

Implicit in this incontestable aspect of human existence is that the human being, and consequently human life, is essentially solitary. The pain and pleasure I feel, the satisfaction I experience when I complete a project I have been working on successfully, the love that swells in my heart in special moments in my life, the hope or cynicism I suffer when I fail now and then, the guilt that festers in my heart when I inadvertently harm another human being or myself, the sickness unto death I endure when I retire from the world of productivity and creation—all these and similar experiences take place in my mind and heart. I can verbally or behaviorally share some of my feelings, ideas, or experiences with a friend, family member, priest, or teacher, but no matter the support or commiseration I receive from others, no matter the depth of support they inspire into my soul, and no matter the kind of communion I have on critical moments in my life such as joy or grief, the exclusiveness and privacy of my inner world retains its status of solitariness.

The experience of solitariness is uncanny, especially when humans cannot directly communicate or commune with other humans, or indirectly with God, or with an artist through their artwork. One feels locked within the walls of one's solitariness. It is an experience of "naked" aloneness. When it is a moment of failure, loneliness, calamity, triumph, or profound love or hate, it "wears" the face of *forlornness*. Its possibility creeps into the soul when the capacity of self-consciousness blooms in the mind of the growing human being at the height of their adolescence. The experience of the self as a subject, or as an independent human reality, entails a state of aloneness because the self discovers that it is developing into an independent reality and that its existence is exclusive of the existence of anything around it. First, the human being comes into the world as a potentiality whose design and realization is their responsibility; second, as a subject, they are enclosed within the solid walls of subjectivity; and third, this subjectivity is the central domain of their existence. In times of danger, fear, anxiety, or alienation from the social world, they hide in the world of their subjectivity.

We frequently envy the rising youth because they are young and because they represent the possibilities and promise of the future—of prosperous life—but we overlook the fact that their life is vitiated with feelings of anxiety, fear, psychological insecurity, uncertainty, contingency, and sometimes confusion, all of which emanate from the experience of solitariness—aloneness. Is it an accident that some young people surrender themselves to the social way of living, that is, to the social herd, rebel against their parents, or distance themselves from the older generation or the "establishment"? Is it an accident that many young people drift in their lives without a purpose or a cause? Is it easy for a young person to create themselves as a subject that thinks, feels, and acts from within? Young people fumble now and then, suffer the pangs of loneliness much of the time, and learn how to discover the capacities that constitute the structure of their humanity before they learn how to stand on their feet as a human individual.

The experience of solitariness is intensified especially when we discover that we are "thrown," "cast," or "abandoned" in a vast universe and sometimes to a social environment that is indifferent to our feelings or existence. This experience is generated by the realization that nature is, first, an alien reality because its mode of existence and structure is radically different from ours, and second, the laws that govern the destiny of natural objects are different from the laws that govern human life. Sometimes, it seems that humanity has fallen on planet Earth from a cosmic spaceship the way contemporary spacecrafts sometimes get lost on our planet. People suppress, surpass, and subjugate the feeling of solitariness by cultivating their social and political nature and by establishing a human environment built in their image, which is an essential feature of living and realizing human destiny, but a reflective, penetrative examination of this destiny, which is a human construct, in which the human mind embraces in a comprehensive grasp the human phenomenon in its manifestations as they reveal themselves in the history of civilization, will certainly disclose a clear consciousness that this mode of existence is one of thrownness, or abandonment. I emphasize this point because consciousness of this fact necessarily provokes a feeling of dependency and along with it a feeling of forlornness.

Is humanity its own master and the architect of its destiny? Even if we grant, or suppose, that the foundation of human existence and destiny is the human essence and that this essence can function as a kind of master, what is its ontological status? On the ground of reality, I exist as the master of my life, and I have no choice about it. Neither does anyone else. To whom am I responsible in the way I conduct my life? Before what bench of law or authority do I justify my existence? Reason? My rational faculty, which is, in principle, imperfect? I may argue that the master that steers the ship of my life is the threefold powers that constitute the structure of my mind. Fine! On what ground does this essence stand and exercise its authority? I am reluctant to invoke a universal power such as the absolute, reason, mind, or the prime mover because such a reality is abstract, metaphysical, and does not seem to show active interest in me or my fellow human beings. Even if it actually exists, I cannot confront it, much less communicate with it with my human language and way of thinking. In the end, if I contemplate my own existence in the privacy of my soul and the light of my life, and in view of the infinity of the universe, can I avoid feeling forlorn in this tremendous, listless, and dreadful infinity?

The point that merits special emphasis at this point of my discussion is that, regardless of the extent to which I can act as the master of my life, how much I can be heroic in prolonging my longevity, and how much I can grow as a human individual, I exist in the world as a solitary being, always provisionally, always contingently, always adventurously, always untethered to a firm ground, always dependent for my being on my natural and social environment. I may assume or in some way cultivate an attitude of self-confidence, of a wise and judicious captain of the ship of my life, and I may behave as if I am invincible in the way I charge into the uncharted land of the future, but no matter how much I am skilled in cultivating this kind of life orientation, from an ontological point of view, I exist in the flow of the cosmic process as a frail, alien, and solitary human being. I come into the world alone, live in it alone, and die in it alone. Broadly, in the realm of ordinary life, some people act as if they are perfect—as if they know how to think, feel, and make the right decisions and act accordingly. But if we remove this garb of perfection they wear, we discover a different kind of reality. The masters of literary, dramatic, poetic, pictorial, and cinematic arts are skilled in removing this garb and presenting a reasonably true picture of human nature.

I am not unaware of the fact that people transcend, that is, break through, the walls of subjectivity in the sense that they open themselves to the human world socially, intellectually, emotionally, practically, and physically—mainly because the human body is an objectification of the human essence as a potentiality—and try to suppress the nagging feeling of solitariness on the one hand and to meet the demands inherent in the impulse to human life on the other. I tend to think that this capacity is the primary power that enables human beings to survive as human individuals and escape from the crunch of solitariness. Does the flight of the artist, the scientist, and the social reformer, as well as the ordinary human being, in their attempt to create and live not express a passion for overcoming the oppressiveness of the walls of subjectivity? But no matter the degree of one's success in flying into the sky of the cosmic process, which is an object of admiration, the human being cannot escape from the immovable walls of solitariness.

THE HUMAN ESSENCE AS AN ABSOLUTE AUTHORITY?

Human beings choose a political system as a human community, for example, democracy, because they desire to be a free people, and they desire to be free people because they want to live under the conditions of goodness, truth, beauty, religiosity, and autonomy. The democratic state provides the necessary and sufficient conditions for the possibility of individual autonomy. The fundamental assumptions that underlie this claim are that (1) the human essence is intrinsically valuable and that (2) human beings are capable of *self-government*. Living under the care, guidance, or auspices of any external power exposes them to the possibility of being treated as objects or instruments and strips them of their most precious possession, namely, humanity, because the essence of their being consists of living in accordance with the values that reflect the primary craving of the impulse to human life.

You seem to absolutize, glorify, and, one can add, divinize the human essence—why, my critic, who has been following the thread of my reasoning, would ask. This absolutization is tantamount to saying that leading an autonomous way of life, or as you have been arguing, a life of self-fulfillment, is human destiny. Is pursuing this destiny worthy of our pursuit? Is it realistic? Leading such a way of life is not easy. Indeed, it involves struggle, hard work, sacrifice, and sometimes crushing pain. Is it advisable, or commendable, to pursue this way of life, in short, if the human being and their achievements will sooner or later vanish as an insignificant ripple in the cosmic process, the way a sandcastle a child builds on the seashore vanishes under the gushing impact of an advancing wave? You seem to suggest that it is appropriate and perhaps justifiable for a human being to design and build a crystal palace, one that attracts the admiration of the gods. Why not lead an easy, carefree way of life, drift in the alleys of social existence, and enjoy a cup of pleasure under the light of the sun once in a while?

These critical questions come from a compassionate heart, a gallant spirit, and a lover of truth. It raises a twofold question of the meaning of human life: How should I live, love, and die? Why should I live, love, and die? Or, articulated more expressively, why do I exist rather than not? The "how" of human existence stems from the "why" of human existence. Although the basis of responding to my critic's query is implicit in the analysis I conducted in the preceding chapter, the following remarks should amplify the warrantability of arguing that the human essence, and as a consequence, (1) human life is intrinsically valuable without endowing it with the absolute right to endure forever and (2) spending a life of painful struggle to exist as a self-determined being is a worthwhile endeavor.

I aver that the human being is an emergent and, like every emergent reality in the cosmic process, it is necessarily a process and so exists as a transient reality. However, this acknowledgment does not trivialize or belittle the value of the human essence, nor does it trivialize the significance of the need to exist and flourish as an autonomous being, despite the fact that the life of the human being is no more than a passing ripple in the cosmic press. This twofold proposition is corroborated by the following elucidating explanation.

First, the thesis I have posited, namely, that the human essence is the highest, noblest, and most refined emergent in the cosmic process, does not necessarily imply that it is absolute in its capacity or that creates itself. It underscores its absolute value in contrast to the value of every other emergent from the cosmic process. The distinctive feature that entitles the human essence to this status of being is its capacity for self-consciousness. This capacity elevates the human being from being an "object" to a "subject," one that is not merely a creature but also a creator. The ability of a human being to create themselves and, more importantly, to create the human world in the process of self-creation is, I suggest, the quintessential characteristic of the divine. Divinity is not necessarily an attribute of a divine being. A being acquires the attribute of divinity by their capacity to create the good, beautiful, true, free, and sacred. It does not matter whether this kind of being endures for a second or for eternity. What matters is that it can create being from nonbeing, especially the highest kind of being. What matters is that its creation shines in the sky of universal being the way the stars shine in the dark sky at night. Would it be whimsical or idle speculation to say that the Absolute that acts as a source and administrator of the cosmic process became conscious of itself as the Absolute in the emergence of human essence from its bosom as a flare of self-consciousness? Is this kind of self-consciousness possible if it is not a creative power and if it does not shine through its creation, that is, if its creation does not reveal the nobility, grandeur, and magnificence of its potential and actual being? It would be strange, if not incomprehensible, to say that the Absolute creates a world worthy of existence if it does not know what it has created, if its creation does not issue from a design that is conscious, thoughtful, purposeful, and volitional, and if it does not recognize itself as an absolute in which it creates?

Second, the human essence does not emerge from the cosmic process as an abstraction, as a positive reality, or as a ready-made object but as a potentiality that inheres in the formal organization of the human body, which is a living reality and, more concretely, as a power primarily because power is the essence of process. As a reality, the process is inconceivable; indeed its existence is impossible if it is not a process of becoming. It is plausible to posit that an object is real inasmuch as it is a process of becoming different from what it is in the present moment. Moreover, the process of becoming is inconceivable without a quantum, or a drop, of power. This quantum inheres in the object as a process of becoming. Accordingly, it would be both unthinkable and impossible for an emergent of any kind of process to be a passive reality but, on the contrary, a *dynamic and powerful reality*. I have emphasized "dynamic" and "powerful" only to emphasize that the emergent reality does not merely possess power or that power is one of its attributes but is power. The word "dynamic" comes from the Greek *dynamis*, which comes from *dynamikos*, "power," which in turn comes from *dynasthai*, "to be able."[1] As a process, a changing object is in a continual state of becoming different from itself; otherwise, the object remains itself. This feature of the human essence is the basis of characterizing it as an impulse. The word "impulse" comes from the Latin *impulsus*, the preposition of *impellere*, which is derived from *in*, "in," and *pellere*, "to drive." An impulse is an impelling or driving forward with sudden force. It also means "a thrust or impetus."[2] As a thrust, it is an impulse to be or to assert its existence by virtue of the dialogical dimension and human existence and flourishing by virtue of its human dimension, that is, human essence.

Accordingly, when we say that the primary impulse in human nature is an impulse to human life, we mean that (1) it exists as a potentiality—otherwise, it would not be an impulse; (2) it is a thrust for being in the future regardless of whether it is near or distant; and (3) it is not a blind or random but a drive for existing as a human being. The question that requires an urgent answer at this juncture of my discussion is, what is the nature of this human potentiality? I have given a general answer to this question in the preceding chapter. The point that merits special emphasis is a response to my critic's query that, as an impulse to human life, it possesses the necessary conceptual and practical resources as well as the means to exist and thrive in the world as a human reality whose structure consists of a process of growth and development. It does not acquire these resources from an external source but has them as elements of its structure; put differently, they are not supervenient on its being but immanent in every fiber of its being. Again, as an impulse in the mode of potentiality, I can add that

1. *Webster's New World College Dictionary*.
2. *Webster's New World College Dictionary*.

the human essence is not only a thrust for human being in the world but also a *cry*, that is, a craving, for such a being.

Unlike the natural objects that make the scheme of nature, which are determined by the logic and laws of the cosmic process, the human essence emerges as a potentiality for realization as an *autonomous being*, one that exists, grows, and develops according to laws innate to its structure. The perfection of the natural object, which lies in realizing the particular essence that gives rise to its identity, is made possible by the forces that steer the nature and direction of the process of its realization. Its perfection is the handiwork of its environment. But the perfection of a particular human essence is the handiwork of the human being as a human individual, that is, as a subject that presides over the substance and direction of its growth and development. This aspect of the human essence is the ontic basis of the intrinsicality of its existence in the sense that humanity is intrinsically valuable. The human being does not derive its value as a reality merely from the fact that it exists as an emergent but from the fact that they are the author of their existence as a human reality. The extent, kind, and measure of the activity in and through which they exist in the world as a human reality is derived from this activity and nowhere else. For example, we commend, laud, and esteem an industrious and productive student, worker in a factory, teacher, artist, farmer, scientist, or parent more than a lazy, mediocre, or unproductive student, teacher, or scientist. More to the point, unlike natural or artifactual objects, which derive their value from the extent to which they are useful, the human being derives their value from the extent to which they grow and develop as a human individual. I am valuable not because I am a biped or a particular lump of flesh but because I am a shining flare of humanity, and the measure of my value in the world is commensurate with the extent of my productivity or human growth and development. This assertion is supported by the generally recognized moral precept that a developing and productive human being is a giving human being. Such a human being gives life in any sphere of practical life. Giving is the essence of love. Miserliness is the essence of selfishness. I spotlight this aspect of the human essence because it reveals the quality of nobility of the human as such. Does the god of theistic religions not reveal its absoluteness in the act of creating the universe and its glory and nobility in the activity of continuously recreating it? Is the act of creation not an act of giving—being and life?

But, as you claim, can the human individual act independently of the laws of nature? my critic would suddenly intervene. Does the human essence not inhere in the formal organization of the human body, which is a natural object, as you have already argued?

The human being necessarily acts in conformity with, or consistently with, the laws of nature, and they cannot act contrary to them, but they can act according to the laws that emanate from their structural constitution. Their being, and the being of the laws according to which they act, emerge from the formal organization of the human body, but the conditions and means of their realization are not subject to the governance of the laws of nature. I emphasize this feature of the human essence to underpin the basis of the claim that it is capable of self-perfection. A being that possesses this power can be qualified with attributes such as "absolute" or "divine." Some of the world's major religions attribute the quality of absoluteness or divinity to the supreme being. Such a being is viewed as perfect not only potentially but also actually. This is why it is characterized by epithets such as infinite, superabundant, boundless, or Absolute (with a capital letter). The word "absolute" comes from the Latin *absolutus*, the preposition of *absolvere*, "to loosen from." Translated into English, it means "perfect, completer, whole."[3] It does not lack anything—of course, anything good. It does not need anything to be what it is. A supreme being cannot coexist with *the* supreme being. Otherwise, it would not be supreme. Only such a being can be conceived as the creator of the universe. In contrast, the human individual is absolute *in potentia*, not *in actus*. The potential aspect of the human essence justifies the commonly recognized claim in ethics and metaphysics that, unlike any other emergent from the cosmic process, perfection, self-completion, or self-realization is the destiny of human beings. But this destiny, which unfolds in the process of daily living, is indeterminate. Its absoluteness or divinity is absoluteness in process or divinity in process. This interpretation of absoluteness is not inconsistent with the religious doctrines of the major religions of the world, according to which "man"—*anthropos*—was created in the image of God. In the present context, the divine image—*imago dei*—signifies "essence," "breath," or "spirit."[4] "Image" cannot merely denote "likeness" because the human essence is finite, and the essence of the Absolute being is infinite. The finite cannot stand in a relation to a comparison with the infinite. However, it is logically

---

3. *Webster's New World College Dictionary*.
4. *Webster's New World College Dictionary*.

and ontologically possible for the infinite being to express essential features of the infinite being or the infinite being to reveal itself in the finite being. As is well known in Roman mythology, Jupiter blew a breath of spirit into the clay Goddess Cura—Goddess of Care—and formed a human being. In this example, essential elements of the absolute are transmitted to the finite.

The greatness and glory of the human essence lie in the fact that it is endowed with the power of self-creation. As I have explained, the secret of this power inheres in the womb of the phenomenon of the human essence as a potentiality. Undermine the possibility of this phenomenon, and you *ipso facto* undermine the existence of the human race. The lion or the apple tree does not worry or feel anxious about its death, even though it struggles to survive, because the means of struggling exist in its essential constitution as instincts and drives. It cannot deviate from them, no matter what happens to it. This is the main reason why animal and botanical organisms do not have a destiny. Their purpose is intertwined with the purpose of the cosmic process. They do not have a design for their life project, much less realize it.

HUMAN DESTINY

Contrary to the generally held belief that the destiny of a living reality, including human reality, is the sequence of the necessary and inevitable events that comprise life of reality, I propose that human beings are, in principle, the authors of their lives: they choose their destiny. The word "destiny" is derived from the Latin *destinare*, "to fasten down, secure."[5] This definition implies that (1) the course of events, regardless of whether they are natural or human, are fixed, determined, or inevitable, and (2) an object is not the author of the laws or sequence of causation that governs the life or duration of the object. This conception of destiny is based on the assumption that human beings are not the authors of their lives and that the course of the activities they perform in their theoretical and practical lives are "fixed" and "determined." But, as I diligently argued in the first chapter, the human dimension of the human being is not given to the world as a ready-made reality but as a reality to be made. The mode of its givenness is the mode of potentiality. Accordingly, if "destiny" signifies the "final end," and the logic and sequence of causation of the events culminate in the realization of the final end, it should follow the human being is the author of their

5. *Webster's New World College Dictionary.*

destiny. I readily acknowledge that, regardless of whether the activities we perform daily are thoughtfully, consciously, and deliberately realized; seem to be performed by habit; or seem to befall us as if we do not choose them, in actuality we choose them by virtue of the fact that we choose the design of our life projects and means of implementing them. The choice of this design originates from our direct immersion in the quiet storm of human existence in the various spheres of human existence on the one hand and the belligerent existence of natural existence on the other. Both natural and social forces are frequent intruders in the course of our lives. The design of a life project that does not take into serious consideration the possibility of this kind of intrusion is neither realistic nor farsighted. As I shall presently argue, individual human life is a work of art. It is an activity of creating a human individual *ex nihilo* the way da Vinci created the *Mona Lisa*. Let me elaborate on this claim in some detail.

The question of human destiny is an extrapolation of the question of how I should live, love, and die, which springs from an indisputable premise that (1) the human essence is given to the world as a potentiality, and the life of the human being consists of the realization of the types we perform daily; and (2) human existence is thrust into the future. We exist in order to live, and our lives are personal tasks. Thus, how should we achieve a life worth living? This question is implied in Socrates's enduring insight that the unexamined life is not worth living. Accordingly, what makes a life worth living? Socrates raised the question because he thought that we are not created simply to exist, in the sense of "to vegetate"; we are created to lead a human way of life. He assumed in raising it that the "I," that is, the part that makes us human, is not the body but a metaphysical entity he called "the soul." As he once remarked, the body is a biped, but as a biped, a human biped is an ensouled body. However, a logical corollary to the question of the unexamined life that is not worth living is what makes a life worth living. Indeed, this question is the reason for writing this book, and the analysis I have been conducting constitutes a philosophical examination of its fundamentals.

An understanding of how I should live, love, and die can be achieved by an understanding of the essential structure and dynamics of the human essence. It is my essence as a human individual being: What is it? What does it want, aspire for, and hope for? Alas! As we have already seen, it (1) exists as a potentiality; (2) its structure consists of three primary capacities, each one of which is an impulse; (3) inherent in these capacities are five peremptory desires that arise from five peremptory needs in the human essence; and (4) the peremptory desires exist as urges, drives, or forces that demand satisfaction or satiation. Their realization is a mode of fulfillment or completion. For example, thirst creates a peremptory need for water. Dehydration signifies a deprivation. I am thirsty. When I drink water, my body feels satiated or satisfied because the activity of satiation arouses a feeling of satisfaction. A body whose needs are satiated is a satisfied body. Similarly, the peremptory desire for truth, goodness, beauty, religiosity, and freedom signifies lack. Feeling this lack generates a demand for satiation. We should always remember that in its mode of living consciousness, as an impulse, the human essence is not merely a cry for being in the world but also a craving for realization or satisfaction. Can the human mind overstep the demands of this cry? Can it desire to be what its nature does not allow? Is giving this nature the opportunity to celebrate the rite of life not its glorious destiny?

TOWARD HUMAN LIVING AS AN ART

The glory and curse of the human being is that they at once exist in the modes of potentiality and reality: their existence is neither exclusively potential nor exclusively real. The secret of this binary nature lies in the fact that the human being exists in the world as an embodied human essence, first, in the formal organization of the human body as a potentiality, and second, in their actions and achievements in the world. In the first place, it comes into being in a state of self-consciousness in the medium of subjectivity. I exist as a concrete reality to myself and nobody else in this medium. I know what it means for me to be a human being when I consciously confront myself in a particular experience. I also confront myself as a being in process. I confront myself as a living reality. In the second place, I come into being as an embodiment in my actions and the works I create and produce, which exist as objects of perception and reflection. I see myself in these objects as a human reality, and people around me also see me as a particular human reality in these objects. Outside the sphere of embodied objects and the sphere of embodiment of other human beings, I exist in the mode of potentiality. As I explained in the preceding chapter, we do not encounter the human phenomenon as a reality existing in and by itself, as a pure human essence, anywhere in the natural or social realms of being. The basis of this dual nature of human existence is the general fact that process is the essence of reality. The ontic locus of the human essence is the formal organization of the human body, which exists in the world as a unique emergent. It depends for its survival on the survival and existence of the body.

The reality that underlies the activity of survival is an intuitive yet rational dialogical negotiation between the human being as a thinking subject and the primary values or their derivatives that exist in the mind on the one hand and the existential conditions in which the impulse to survive is active on the other. The conceptual structure of this negotiation can be articulated in the following form: How can I maximize the highest possible measure of human satisfaction in the present moment? How can I expand and deepen the human dimension of my being, which exists in my reflection as an inexhaustible possibility of realization in the present existential situation? The human essence comes to life in this kind of negotiation, which is an ongoing process, mainly because my life is an ongoing process. The existential challenge, which constantly hovers around the rim of my consciousness in the process of human living, is our inmost impulse to maximize human satisfaction. But how can we achieve this demand of the human impulse for human survival? Or, how can we live, love, and die from the standpoint of the realized values that constitute the fabric of our character? I submit that a necessary condition for meeting this demand is acting as an *artist* in translating the values that are the foundation of human existence into productive action and creation. I have called attention to "artist" to emphasize that translating human values into action is not a skill, nor is it habitual in character, but it is art at its best. It stands on par with any fine art. An examination of this claim should, I think, begin with an adequate understanding of the fundamental assumption that human self-realization is an activity of self-creation. The following section will be devoted to an analysis of this central idea of human existence. The following chapter shall be devoted to the thesis that the activity of self-creation is art par excellence.

CHAPTER FOUR

A Life Worth Living as Art

THE BASIS OF HUMAN LIFE AS ART

The time is now ripe to ask, Iin what sense is authentic human life—the kind that originates from the values that function as the foundation of human life—art, or under what existential conditions can a human being live a life worth living? More to the point, is the claim that leading a human way of life justifiable? I propose that this is the most important philosophical question, more important than asking about the nature of the power that underlies the creation and existence of the universe, the nature of political systems, beauty, the principles of moral behavior, the method of establishing the truth of our knowledge of nature and human nature, or the nature of human genius. On the contrary, these and related questions are important *both theoretically and practically because answering them adequately is a means, if not the necessary condition, to a reasonableexistential answer to the question of what makes a life worth living*: How should I live as a human being? I assume in making this assertion that we do not seek to know merely because we are curious or desire to know but to live, to live well, to live better—hopefully always better. The attainment of knowledge is not the ultimate end of human existence. Authentic life—this way of life is the ultimate source of the most important kind of satisfaction the human mind and heart crave. Every type of pleasure, enjoyment, or gratification derives its significance from this primary satisfaction mainly because it is their source. Suppose I stand naked before the mirror of truth and ask myself the following simple question: You have been striving to acquire knowledge, social acceptance and approval, divine grace, and to perform with diligence family, social, and political duties. Suppose you have been indulging in some pleasures now and then, and finally, suppose you have been cultivating meaningful friendships, engaging pleasant hobbies, and most of all, striving to be a successful professional who commands the respect and admiration of your peers and superiors. Now, if you reflect on the stream of your adventures, actions, and accomplishments in the course of your short life, you have to admit that it was a serious labor and frequently intimidating, frustrating, anxious, depressing, painful, and torturously lonely.

Next, suppose, having sailed through the threatening, turbulent, and anxious, as well as the peaceful, joyful, and triumphant moments of your life, you suddenly find yourself standing at the Edge—the edge of all edges—of your life, when every organ in your body weakens, especially the intellectual and emotional powers of your mind. Suppose you reflect on the kind of life you have lived, and suddenly the question of all questions in your life assumes the figure of Master Doubt. He sits on the fringe of your consciousness with a critical, if not a sarcastic, grin on his lips. By the way, the grin of this master cannot be avoided. Sarcasm is the quintessence of his nature. It is a speaking grin, and it is loud and clear: "Is the life you have lived justifiable?" With a frown on your forehead, you retort, "Justifiable?"

"Yes!" Master Doubt answers with an ironic wrinkle in his grin—"Justifiable! Are you proud of it? Was it the right kind?"

"I lived it!"

"A child can answer my question the way you did. Was the life you lived worth living?"

Baffled, I respond, "I never asked myself this question."

"Do you mean you've lived it without wondering why or how you've lived it? Do you mean you have lived it the way the cat or butterfly lives their life?"

The furrows on my head deepen. Master Doubt, whose eyes grasped the significance of those furrows, replaces the sarcastic grin on his lips with an expression of compassion and then continues his line of questioning.

"You have been in your personal, professional, religious, and social life an astute, discriminating person. You know the difference between right and wrong, good and bad, beauty and ugliness. Was the life you have lived the best you could have imagined? Was it better, equal, or worse than the life other people in your community lived or still live?"

"I did my best!"

"How do you know you have done your best? It cannot be the best if it is not good. What makes a life good, better, or best? What makes a life good or bad?"

The hedges of the furrows on my head thicken, and the hawkish eyes of Master Doubt notice a few drops of sweat shimmering between them. My heart throbs fast and hard. I stare at the devil behind those compassionate eyes. Master Doubt is my tormentor, or perhaps my ally. How can the voice of truth be the voice of an enemy?

A justifiable human life is a life worth living, and a life worth living is, as I discussed in the last two chapters, a life lived in accordance with the values that emanate from human essence. How would you characterize this kind of life? my critic would ask. Every person around you would say that theirs is a life worth living! Some may add that their lives are models of human living. Is there a measure for determining the nature of a life that is worth living?

First, I readily acknowledge that a finally established measure, similar to some measures in mathematics or science, is not possible. It is possible for a measure to assume a formal, theoretical, or logical validity, but it will resist finality on the ground of reality because human life is a subjective reality and so unobservable empirically. Accordingly, it is difficult to ascertain the depth, truth, or quality of a life; moreover, the material and spiritual conditions under which people live are variable in kind and significance. However, we can articulate a philosophical principle of explanation that serves as a basis for understanding, evaluating, and justifying the possibility of a life worth living. Such a principle should be logically and ontologically plausible. The criterion of its plausibility is the extent to which it is founded on a reasonable conception of human nature, which I advanced in the first chapter, and an adequate analysis of the values that emanate from it as a response to the peremptory needs that inhere in the human essence as an impulse to human life. This proposal is based on the fundamental assumption that, regardless of whether it is animal, physical, or human, the destiny of any object consists of existing and realizing itself according to the logic and laws inherent in its essential structure. For example, an apple tree is good inasmuch as it produces the highest possible grade of apple; a rock is good inasmuch as it functions as a building block, weapon, or a sculpture; or a lion is good in as much as it thrives in the wild without violating the natural or biological environment in which it roams.

Similarly, the life of a human being is worth living inasmuch as it is lived from the core of human essence. What are the dynamics of this essence? If this essence is an impulse to human life, if it defines the humanity of the human being, if its realization consists of meeting the existential demands of the peremptory needs inherent in its structure, which I discussed in chapter two, it would follow that maximizing the realization of these values in the life of the individual is not merely the substance of one's destiny in this short life of ours but especially the fact that makes life worth living.

Practically, the evaluation of a life's worthiness cannot be done at the beginning or middle of one's life but, as Aristotle recommended, at its end. Only then can a human being stand before the mirror of truth, contemplate the life they lived, and then judge whether it was worth living. Was it lived in accordance with the values of truth, goodness, beauty, religiosity, and individuality? Does the way a person lived reflect an adequate understanding of these values? Standing before this mirror is, in effect, standing before the bench of one's conscience—the ultimate judge of one's life's worthiness. However, no matter how personal, subjective, or private it may be, it reveals itself through its actions and achievements. Although human subjectivity, as I have already argued, is windowless, being a center of being, its mode of existence in the world is one of objectification or embodiment; it becomes real or conceivable in what it does. Outside the realm of its objectifications or embodiments, it remains in the state of potentiality. This is why, although a human being who stands before the mirror of truth may evaluate their life as great or well lived, they may be mistaken in their evaluation before the mirror of reason. The criterion of truth for human reason is individual and communal well-being, that is, the extent to which a human being promotes the greatest possible measure of happiness or human well-being in their own life and in the lives of others.

Lest someone wonder about the warrantability of this conclusion, I should emphasize that it is not drawn hastily. I beg my reader to focus attention on (1) the fact that the human essence inheres in the formal organization of the body as a potentiality and, therefore, no matter what it does or produces in the world, it is always an embodied reality; (2) this potentiality comes to life as a concrete reality in human experience and nowhere else; (3) the human body is essentially a process and, as such, a temporal reality that comes into being at a certain point in time and passes out of being at a later point in time; (4) we grant, as we should, that the human being is a finite reality in the sense that they are a windowless subjectivity and necessarily exist in the world as a solitary being; and (5) we recognize that human life is a thrust into the future and therefore exists in the world as a process of becoming—yes, yes, if we contemplate the meaning of these aspects of human existence, we can justifiably ask not only, Why do I exist but, more importantly, How should I live and love in this short life of mine?

Moreover, the justifiability of this question acquires a high degree of importance, indeed urgency, when, as an instance of humanity, I stand before the mirror of truth and direct my attention to the fact that my existence is intrinsically good and realize that my life is short, I do not only *tremble* because it is short but also feel an *obligation* to cherish it and live it with a deep feeling of respect and appreciation. I have emphasized "tremble" and "obligation" because, first, my life is good, at least to me, and because the good should not perish, I should not perish; and second, it is immoral, and I can add contrary, to my nature to waste or desecrate the good. Of course, I can commit suicide; drift into the dark alleys of social existence as a nomad; or eat, drink, and be merry because tomorrow may never come. Why? If we examine the demands this question implies, we discover that the existential conditions of human existence, which include a lack of education, poverty, ignorance, injustice, bigotry, oppression, and selfishness, among other negative factors, stand in the way of meeting the conditions for human growth and development. But the point that calls for special attention is the need to lead a human way of life, which is innate to the human essence as an impulse to human life. I don't exaggerate if I say that the inmost aspiration of this essence is to exist, grow, and develop from within, that is, from the values that emanate from the impulse to human life.

Your plea to live, love, and die on the basis of a distinct consciousness of the fact that human life is short, painful, my critic would now intervene, and especially the fact that, regardless of the extent to which it is mediocre, poor, successful, or great, the life of the human being is, in the final analysis, a passing ripple in the cosmic process. What is wrong with a life of "eating, drinking, and being merry" if the life is no more than a passing ripple in the cosmic process so that it will pass into the world of eternal oblivion sooner than one can begin to enjoy it? Moreover, is it not *morbid* for a human being to live with the consciousness that death is around the corner?

These two questions reveal some of the most wearisome, if not unsettling, aspects of human existence. I doubt that any sage, scientist, or philosopher can give a universally satisfying answer or absolutely valid answer primarily because, metaphysically, the essence of natural and human reality is an indecomposable composite of change and permanence—of being and nonbeing. Any reality begins to perish the moment it comes into being. This fact applies to human and natural realities. It is an instantiation of the supreme law of existence: change. But although human existence is an instantiation of this supreme law, it does not necessarily stand in the way of assuming a positive and constructive attitude toward the need to lead a human way of life. Let me elaborate on and defend the following proposition in some detail: despite the fact that (1) human life is short, (2) leading a human way of life involves painful striving, and (3) the achievements of human beings will be buried in the graveyard of oblivion, it is, I submit, both desirable and justifiable to assert that human beings should do their best to promote their human growth and development and the growth and development of others and that it shortsighted, if not foolish, to neglect one's growth and development.

First, I am not the author of my existence. I discover that I am a human being existing in the world in a certain geographical and cultural place at a certain period of human civilization. Accordingly, I am not, in principle, the author of my destiny as a given and particular essence; on the contrary, my destiny is implicitly given to me as a potentiality for realization. However, I am the author of the process of realizing my essence, given the natural and human environment in which I discover myself as a human being. Can I choose to be a rock, a tree, or a cat? Can I choose to be born here rather than there, or at this rather than that time? But I can choose to be a bright flare of human life and delight in the mystery of the cosmic process, and more importantly, I can sizzle the joy of self-creation and the continual creation of the human and natural world around me. If I express this point metaphorically, I can view my existence as an invitation to celebrate the rite of human life, which is not only a distinctive type of experience but also an intrinsically valuable gift. Do I have the right to denigrate or belittle the supreme significance of this gift? What if I am invited to a banquet that offers the best food and drink, most refined guests, most elevating music, and most delightful conversation—do I have the right to complain when it is time for me to bid my host goodbye? In contrast, am I not expected to conduct myself appropriately and avail myself of the experience I undergo during this event? The answer to the question of why I should strive to maximize the realization of myself as a human being lies in the fact that the essence, which is the source of my humanity and my existence, is given to the world as an impulse to human life.

Second, the plea to lead a human way of life on the basis of understanding the ontological basis of human existence—namely, finitude, transience, and potentiality—does not necessarily imply that every day when we wake up in the morning or every time we need to make a decision about a prospective action, we should be conscious of our finitude or the fact that death is waiting around the corner. It only means that our life project should be designed and implemented on the principle, or fact, that we are finite and mortal. It also means that we should not live as if we are immortal. It is sad to note that many people discover this mistake only when they retire or when they are victims of a fatal disease, accident, or calamity. They devote their time and spiritual resources to amassing wealth, fame, power, or knowledge as if these achievements will endure, not knowing that they will be buried in the belly of oblivion. I aver that good achievements endure, but sadly, they endure for a limited time only. We remember and sometimes acknowledge our indebtedness to the great scientists, philosophers, theologians, artists, and social reformers, but their remembrance and the impact of their achievements do not withstand the forces of perishing.

HUMAN LIFE AS ART

The question of how I should live, love, and die arises because (1) my life and I are not given as ready-made realities, (2) I am responsible for realizing my essence and living my life, and (3) my existence is an unstoppable thrust into the future. If I am allowed to express myself plainly or bluntly, I can say that I am stuck between two invincible events—my birth and death. The proposition I shall elucidate and defend in the following pages is that leading a human way of life, that is, designing my life project and implementing it in the course of daily existence, is an art. Accordingly, an authentic human being is an artist of human living.

As a society, we tend to packoverload the minds of rising youth with a large load of academic stuff. For example, we teach them the basic ideas of physics, biology, geology, mathematics, philosophy, art, politics, anthropology, religion, social sciences, chemistry, and related academic disciplines. We also fill their minds with practical skills such as business, medicine, law, farming, soldiering, and engineering, and to a lesser extent, we teach them the rudiments of the fine arts such as music, painting, sculpture, or architecture. This academic and practical stuff unfortunately does not automatically, if not miraculously, translate into an intuitive knowledge or skill in how to live a life worth living. It is a necessary but not sufficient condition for mastering the art of human living.

But knowing the basic principles and ideas of the sciences and arts, regardless of whether they are theoretical or practical, is one thing, and knowing the conditions of translating this knowledge into a human way of thinking, feeling, and acting is something else. Ideas are abstract; as such, they are impotent. They exist in the mind as mental states. The question is, How can an idea become a principle of action? How can the truth it embodies animate, that is, give life to an action we intended to perform? The knowledge the youth acquires when they receive their education in school, or in the institutions of society, is a necessary condition for acting rationally, or in accordance with the values that emanate from human essence, but it is not a sufficient condition for knowing how to chart and lead a human way of life.

For example, you do not become a heart surgeon simply by reading certain books in physics, chemistry, mathematics, psychology, and biology, nor by reading books that explain step-by-step the procedures for treating heart diseases, although this and related kinds of knowledge are a necessary condition for becoming skilled in performing heart surgery. You become a heart surgeon by learning how to apply the ideas and principles in concrete, individual heart maladies or malfunctions, that is, by cultivating the skill of how to treat such maladies or malfunctions. The skill is acquired by training, and the training is acquired by doing: first, by observing a master surgeon in the act of performing heart surgeries and, second, by experience or by doing under the supervision of the master surgeon. Thinking is one kind of activity, and doing is a different kind of activity; or, put differently, theory is one kind of activity, and practice is a different kind of activity. However, it is possible for a person to acquire a certain kind of skill without possessing the theoretical knowledge underlying it or functioning as its basis, for example, farming, midwifery, or soldiering. You can be a good midwife, farmer, or soldier without knowing the physical, mathematical, chemical, or biological ideas, theories, or assumptions of any of these skills. The manifold types of activities we conduct in the course of our daily lives are performed skillfully, sometimes poorly and other times competently. We frequently acquire a variety of practical skills in the process of conducting the business of living by imitation, guidance, or trial and error. But, regardless of its kind, a skill is cultivated by practice.

One distinctive feature of skill is that once it is established, its practice virtually becomes repetitive; it implies regularity and continuity of the existential conditions in which it is practiced. For example, as a carpenter, I may be skilled in making a certain type of chair. Given the material necessary to make it, I can make the same chair as long as needed. My skill is limited to this kind of making. Moreover, I can act, or function, as a master carpenter. In this case, I can teach other people how to make different kinds of chairs. The master knows not only the principles and the nature of the materials they use in making a certain kind of chair, but they also know the possibilities inherent in the essential structure of the materials as well as their design possibilities. Every kind of wood possesses specific features and therefore different possibilities of realization. These features and possibilities are discovered in the process of forming the material in certain functional ways. As an apprentice, I watch how my master makes a kind of chair and try to glean how they know or discover the possibilities of different kinds of wood. The point that merits special emphasis here is that a skill is acquired or cultivated by imitation and practice. Does this imply that a chair, for example, cannot be a work of art? No necessarily. As I shall momentarily explain, art is a creative process *sui generis*. It implies skill, but it is much more than skill.

LIVING A LIFE WORTH LIVING IS NOT A SKILL

The human being is the life they live. Their being, which is a process, unfolds in the activities they perform daily from the moment they open their eyes to the world in the morning to the moment they surrender their consciousness to Morpheus, god of sleep. These activities, which are physical, social, professional, and spiritual, can be subsumed under the category of "action." They may be trivial, important, momentous, long, or short, and they may have different kinds of qualities, depending on the kinds of values or purposes they express or reveal—for example, religious, moral, or aesthetic value. The majority of the activities we perform daily are done mechanically, routinely, and sometimes repetitiously, but frequently habitually. Although the way most of these and similar types of actions are ingrained in the mind as inclinations and attitudes, they are not thoughtless or nonrational but, as John Dewey argued some time ago, intelligent because they are acquired on the basis of a consciously and rationally conceived kind of behavior. Acting habitually frees us from the task of examining and evaluating the meaning of every minor activity we have to perform—of course, most of the time.

But regardless of whether they are major or minor, significant or insignificant, simple or complex, long or short, a large number of the activities that comprise the life of the human being on the ground of reality are kinds of skills. Although habitually done, these activities are done skillfully. We may view habit as a skill. As such, it is an ingrained mode of behavior. It performs this function in two ways: first, as an established disposition and, second, as a *schema*. What is in fact ingrained is the form or structure of the activity, not the activity itself. A habitual action is an appropriation of the activity to the ingrained form or schema. Once the activity is performed, it moves into the bank of memory as an individual event. Walking, eating, bathing, socializing, driving a car, reading, writing, swimming, and sometimes thinking or expressing ourselves in a certain way are habitual modes of behavior. These and similar activities are instantiations of ingrained schemas or forms of action. The schema lingers in the memory as a skeleton, but the content of the action, that is, the particular event, is most of the time forgotten, of course, unless the action happens to be momentous.

Although the majority of the actions we perform in the course of our daily lives, in the sphere of family, social, religious, and professional experience, are habitual—or even semi-habitual—they require thought, deliberation, and frequently choice. Again, not all habitual behavior is mechanical or merely repetitive, mainly because the practical conditions in which we find ourselves are often novel, challenging, and sometimes transcend the boundaries of established habit. For example, as a liberal arts teacher, I am in the habit of counseling my students academically and, on certain occasions, on personal matters. I am skilled in performing this task by welcoming the student, making them feel comfortable, and being willing to communicate with them. Consultants in the areas of sociology and psychology are skilled in this counselling. Some of the counselling cases are easy or technical, while others are serious, complicated, grave, or unique. No two human beings or two human situations are exactly alike. When I find myself in this kind of situation, I suspend the habitual way of counselling. I ask myself, How can I give this student the best advice? Acting in the capacity of counselor is a moment of creative decision-making and acting in two ways: first, I have to evaluate the elements of the situation, which is strictly individual, and then articulate advice that may be helpful to the student, and second, in helping them, I perform a good action, one in which I realize myself as a professional and as a human being.

But the majority of the actions we perform in the course of our practical lives are activities of self-realization, not only because they are novel creations but especially because they are human: they are moments of human growth. Novelty is an essential feature of creation in the realm of nature or the cosmic process because every emergent in this process is necessarily novel in the sense that it comes into existence for the first time. However, what is created, or what emerges, in the natural or cosmic process is an extension of the natural process and happens according to its laws. However, what is created by human beings is an extension of the human essence—of its inner dynamic, logic, and laws. It does not happen according to the laws of nature, although it happens consistently with them. Its mode of creation is *sui generis* par excellence. Regardless of its significance or kind, human action is essentially a creative act. No one can design or implement the design except the human individual. I shall now discuss in great detail the question of self-realization and self-creation and then explain the sense in which the human individual creates, and recreates, themself in every action they perform in the course of their life.

QUESTION OF SELF-REALIZATION AND SELF-CREATION

The preceding analysis of the implications that the human essence exists as a potentiality in the formal organization of the human body, namely, the impulse to life, finitude, and solitariness, will clearly show that, as a type of reality, the human being is a being in process or in a constant state of becoming. No matter its kind, duration, or degree of significance, every moment I confront myself in the event of self-self-consciousness, I confront a reality in process whose existence is unfolding into my next state of being. Although it is not an integral part of the natural process, its existence is subject to the supreme law of reality, namely, change, because it inheres in the formal organization of the human body, which is an integral part of this process. As an emergent from this process, one that surpasses in its essential structure the structure of any other type of emergent, its being must necessarily consist of self-creation. This proposition is based on the fact that, unlike natural objects that emerge as ready-made realities, the human essence, that is, the human being, emerges as a potentiality that is inherently capable of self-creation. As I argued in the first part of this chapter, it is the kind of emergent that is equipped with the capacity and the resources to realize itself concretely as an individual reality, namely, the capacity to envision or conceive a plan and create the means of realizing it, as well as the will to translate the plan into action. But the urgent question the human being faces the moment they see the light of day as an independent reality, which arises from the impulse to life and exists as a pre-reflective sense in the bosom of the impulse, is, How should I be, and more concretely, how should I live? How can the human potentiality move from a state of indeterminacy into a state of determinacy that can exist in the world as a human individual? I have discussed the logical and ontological dynamics of the process involved in the growth and development of the human individual, namely, the concretization of the human essence into the capacities of thinking, affection, and volition. They are determinations of the human essence *qua* power. Each one functions as an urge, that is, as a peremptory desire that aims to meet peremptory needs inherent in the structure of the human essence. The criterion on the basis of which the peremptory needs are met necessarily leads to the articulation of five primary values: truth, beauty, goodness, religiosity, and freedom.

However, the conceptualization of the process necessary for the realization of the human essence as a human individual is not enough, mainly because the conceptual structure is theoretical and acts as (1) a principle of explanation and (2) a guidepost that illuminates the method the individual employs in realizing themselves as a human being. Let us suppose that in the activity of growing and developing as a human being, either personally or with the help of parents, friends, teachers, or counselors, they discover the significance and viability of the theoretical and practical conditions of living according to the logic and demands inherent in the human essence. Still, they need to know the "how" or practicable conditions under which they can grow as the person they aim to be. How can they transform the potentiality that exists in the formal organization of their body into a mature human being so that the transformation results not in a ready-made human individual but in an individual whose being is "being in process," primarily because, like everything that exists, process is the defining feature of the being? It is always a thrust into the next, yet new, moment, which is always different from the preceding moment because the conditions of their natural and social environment are constantly changing. They cannot reflect on the state of their identity in the succeeding moment of their existence because they have to appropriate the existential conditions of the new moment of their existence. In the process of appropriation, they cannot get assistance from anyone because no one can render such assistance. Even if they receive assistance from a sage, teacher, parent, or counselor, they are the sole person who can transform the potential into action. The activity of decision-making, especially when the situation is serious or decisive, takes place in the privacy of one's soul—alone. The sage, teacher, or counselor can show me how to write my paper, but they cannot write it. The only paper they can write is their paper. The domain of "my," "mine," "me," or "I" is neither transferrable nor repeatable. Regardless of whether it is individual or communal, an action is always an individual responsibility because it issues from a particular mind. The sphere in which that which is ideal in nature is miraculously transformed into a concrete reality is a human experience. This kind of transformation is an activity of creation because the dimension of reality that emerges in the process of living is creativity *par excellence*. The practical is a lived reality. Again, that which is human comes into being as a lived reality. Its medium is, as I argued in the first part of this chapter, in the human experience and nowhere else. In all its manifestations, humanity exists in the mode of potentiality and comes to life in the experience of a human being.

Conformists, drifters, and people who lead the life of the social herd, my critic would now interject, can hardly recognize, much less claim, that they are the creators of their lives, and they can hardly comprehend the assertion that their lives are activities of self-creation. They grow and develop in a particular social environment and, in some way, discover that they are mature human beings. All they have to do is simply eat; drink; socialize; work; go to school where they learn intellectual, professional, or emotional skills; and try their best to enjoy a few morsels of pleasure now and then. Their kind of life can easily be characterized as mechanical. I doubt that they are aware of the fact that they are creators, much less self-creators, and I doubt that they know what it means for their lives to be activities of self-creation. Is it possible for an activity to be creative if the subject that presides over its design is not conscious that their action is an activity of creation? Again, are ordinary people the architects and engineers of their lives? How can they be such architects if they are conformists? Can we say that a young person who is not yet conscious of themselves as a subject is a self-created being? Are they not a product of their environment?

This critical line of reasoning is a request to explain the sense in which the human being is a process of self-creation. The tree or the rock is a process of creation mainly because it is a part of the cosmic process; it is not the subject that oversees or directs the destination of its process. Thus, given the fact that some human beings either drift in the alleys of the social herd or lead the life of a human herd, which is a community of human individuals, can we justifiably say that their lives are processes of self-creation?

Let me at once submit that, regardless of whether they are a well-rounded human individual or a skilled conformist; regardless of whether they are a great scientist, artist, or philosopher; and regardless of whether they are a dull, indolent, or unproductive functionary, the life of a human being is a process of self-creation. This proposition is a fundamental assumption that underlies the analysis I am conducting in this discourse. It is warranted by the fact that the human essence (1) exists as a potentiality in the formal organization of the human body, (2) is always a single or individual reality, (3) exists concretely as an embodied reality, (4) is temporal, (5) is essentially a value reality, and (6) its being, or life, is not transferrable. Accordingly, if human life is a living flare of human existence, if it emanates from the human essence as a particular individuality, it should follow that it is an ongoing process of self-creation in the sense that it renews itself as a new individual in every next experience it undergoes.

Given these six features of human existence, the following questions necessarily arise: How should I live, love, and die? Under what conditions can the life I lead be worth living? How can I justify it? I assume, in raising these questions, that (1) human life is intrinsically valuable because the human essence is intrinsically valuable and (2) the realization of human potentiality is an activity of creation. Accordingly, its creation is an activity of self-creation. How can I translate the values of truth, goodness, beauty, religiosity, and freedom, which exist in my mind as general concepts, ideals, or schemas, into concrete living actions in the course of my daily life? Alas! By what magic can the translation of an abstract concept of beauty, goodness, or truth acquire a concrete, living reality in my life? Or, how can action, which exists in the world as a natural event, embody a human quality such as goodness, beauty, or truth? For example, how can the beauty the artist embodies in their work come to life as a world of meaning in the aesthetic experience? This thread of questions calls for the following comments.

A Life Worth Living as Art

Every human experience we undergo in our lives is a moment of potential development because the realization of human value as meaning widens and deepens the human dimension (mind) of the human being. The meaning that we apprehend and enjoy, which finds its way into our minds, does not move into the mind but gets assimilated or incorporated into its structure. It enhances the power of thinking, feeling, and desiring. For example, the more I love, the more I grow in the capacity of love; the more I perform acts of courage, the more I become courageous; and the more I seek the being of God, the closer I move to him. Now, if, as I shall momentarily discuss, human life is a thrust into the future, if a vision of the future is forbidden to us, the question that piques my curiosity is, How can I make a sound judgment or perform a good action that will unfold in my life in the near or distant future? Should I not assume that articulating such a judgment or planning such an act requires the mind of an "artist" and the will of a creative intellect?

You seem to slide into the lap of romantic idealism, my critic would intervene at this point of my discussion. Do you imply that the people who populate the social world are, now and in the past, artists of human living? They are human beings, and they live as human beings. You appear to argue that if one is a human being, and if being human is an activity of self-creation, then people are necessarily artists of human living. But if we cast an inquiring look at the way people live in different parts of the world, we do not encounter artists of human living; on the contrary, we encounter "social herds," an invisible "they" which lurks actively on the fringes of the different societies of the world and assumes the character of a "shepherd." It seems to manage the way the members of the herd live. This shepherd concretely acts in the name of a firmly established system of norms, beliefs, conventions, customs, traditions, practices, and rites, even the way the members eat, drink dress, or fulfill their collective and personal needs. If you permit me to borrow an expression from Socrates in his last dialogue with Crito, before he drank the poison, I can add that this shepherd acts as a militant *public opinion*. It is more militant than social reformers and critics tend to think. The moment a child is born, they are initiated into the life of the social herd. When they grow and gradually discover that their character is already formed, they also discover that the conditions of the way of living is generally charted by the invisible shepherd. I grant that, like a shepherd, they have some freedom in how to conduct theirlife, but this freedom is limited by the resources and conditions of survival. If you reflect on how people live with the eyes of a seasoned hawk, you will, in general, see that people in every society generally think, feel, and act similarly, given the differences in their genetic, material, educational, and material resources. Is it appropriate to say they act similarly to the way bees act? Oh, yes, some members of the herd deviate from the established way of living, but these people are frequently alienated. They are treated as eccentric, strange, abnormal, strays, and sometimes failures. Broadly, conformity, not creativity, and certainly not creative individualism, seems to be the dominant feature of social life throughout the world.

I grant that all human beings, regardless of the degree to which they conform to the established way of living, assume, at least formally, responsibility for their actions and act as if they are the masters of their lives. But are they? If they are, to what extent? How can they be such masters if they receive their beliefs, values, way of acting, even their character and ways of living, from the same shepherd? Can you explain the sense in which self-realization is self-creation? In what sense is self-creation an art? Moreover, how can one lead a life worth living in a society of conformists?

This stream of perceptive and caring questions, first advanced by Socrates in the fifth century BC and reaching a high point of critical evaluation by philosophers and artists in the middle of the twentieth century, remains a viable challenge to any advocate of the human way of life. Indeed, this challenge merits serious attention, especially in view of the increasing dominance of the contemporary, economic, technological, and political forces on the one hand and the gradual transformation of humanistic values propounded by the social reformers that dominated the life of Western societies during the past centuries on the other hand. The values of naive hedonism, superficial individualism, selfishness, economic success, and contentment in a secure, mediocre life seem to replace the values that express and satisfy the inmost cravings for serious beauty, truth, and moral progress. However, I am cognizant of the cry of the human essence for satisfaction that resists silencing, as well as the forces that tend to counteract the intellectual, cultural, educational, and political conditions that foster the possibility of this satisfaction. The wheels of moral, political, intellectual, artistic, and cultural progress seem to move onward slowly, ever so slowly, in the march of history. Nevertheless, I am confident that the fire of the human spirit cannot be quenched. I am also confident that every civilizational step forward we make is an introduction to a more productive and constructive step of human development. I cannot corroborate this confidence with absolute certainty scientifically or syllogistically, but I cling to it on the basis of a long, sustained, synoptic, and contemplative yet critical reflection on the course of human civilization during the past five millennia. Can any observer of the course of human history either ignore or berate the amazing progress of human civilization? Can anyone deny that the more we understand the nature of physical and human reality, the more we advance in our ability to build a more human world? Not only the artist, in their studio or in their silent struggles, fumbles, and frustrations, learnings, and triumphs, but the scientist in their laboratory, the philosopher in the privacy of their soul, and the social reformer in the turbulent ocean of political life face the challenges of human creation and progress patiently and valiantly.

I readily agree with my critic that many people in the world seem to lead the herd way of life, but it would be a grave mistake to support or assent to its accuracy or to the validity of its claim. First, even if we assert that the majority of human beings throughout the world tend to lead the herd way of life, we should grant that this was designed to meet the peremptory needs inherent in the human essence and that this design was conceived consciously, thoughtfully, and creatively. It does not matter how this design differs from one society to another, one historical period to another, or in different geographical or cultural conditions: what matters is that an examination of these ways of living in the different parts of the world—regardless of whether they are nomadic, feudal, monarchic, or democratic—will show that these ways were designed and implemented thoughtfully and creatively. The new generations of the diversity of human society are always beneficiaries of their forebears. However, an established way of life does not necessarily imply that the way of life is not erected on a creatively designed foundation that may be poor or highly rational.

Moreover, even if human beings tend to conform to the established norms, traditions, customs, practices, beliefs, and values of society, we should recognize that this way is dynamic mainly because the spiritual and material conditions of life are constantly changing and frequently developing. Accordingly, I should at once admit that the reverse of this tendency of human life is an integral aspect of human civilization. A quick look at the process of this history from its inception to the present will readily show that it is the history of rising and falling cultures, religions, societies, political systems, and ways of life. But despite this mysterious, disturbing, and baffling feature of the history of human life, I am inclined to think that *sub specie universalis*, the history of the human species is a movement toward a higher state of being. Individuals, societies, cultures, or ways of living rise and fall, but the flame of the human essence cannot vanish as long as the human body endures. Its dynamics are always inventive, progressive, and expansive in its capacity to realize the depth of its being.

Second, let us grant, as my critic stated, that a large multitude of people in different parts of the world are conformists; still, creativity is either necessary or a necessary condition for making the major decisions they perform in the course of their daily lives. Unlike the actions of animals, which take place according to the laws of nature, the actions of human beings take place according to the laws of the human essence. How? First, human action is thrust into the next moment, no matter its length, and second, it is always individual. The value, norm, purpose, or rule according to which the action is designed exists in the mind as a general abstract mental reality. Its precept, meaning, or plan cannot fortuitously jump from the mind and transform itself into a particular action in the life of the human being, even if the being has performed similar actions in their past. The conditions of life are constantly new and always different. More importantly, performing a serious action requires a conception of the value or norm as a schema and translating its precept or meaning into a particular action. This activity is congenitally creative. Human beings are no automata; they are human actors. I am aware of the fact that much of what people do in our practical life is habitual—routine, almost mechanical. But, first, even if it seems mechanical or ingrained as a way of acting, it is inherently intelligent. It is established on the basis of a successful manner of acting. Habitual action is essentially purposeful. It necessarily requires the need to translate the purpose or value into a living activity. This kind of activity is, at least to a modest degree, creative.

I may hastily expose myself to the charge that I am supporting or defending the herd way of life if I say that an established way of leading a human way of life is a necessary condition for the possibility of creative human living because it serves as a primary resource for the human individual to live as an autonomous human being. But this charge is inapplicable. Can I live as a human being, much less grow and develop, if I do not possess the skills needed to meet the ordinary activities of my life? Does society not institutionalize the conditions for creative reaction? The pillars of creativity in human experience are the values that emerge from the human essence. Should we not treat these values as the foundation of our lives or as our ultimate object of love and desire in the process of developing our humanity? These values are the foundation of human civilization. They are, moreover, the basis of the institutions in which we live, and they are also the basis of the way we live. The more the scope of cognitive, moral, aesthetic, religious, and political actions are instantiations of these values, the greater the possibility of creative action. What is especially important is that they are the ultimate source of creative action in science, philosophy, art, religion, and ordinary life. If we examine the root of any action we seek, regardless of whether it is theoretical or practical, we can trace it to a particular value!

The point that calls for special attention in this context is that human existence is a process of continual change—of passing into and out of being. Unlike natural objects, which repeat the essential structure of their identity in every moment of coming into being and passing out of being, human beings have to create themselves in every next moment of their life primarily because they do not exist, for example, the way rocks exist, as ready-made objects. They recreate themselves in two ways: first, in resuming their existence and second, in developing as individuals in and through the concrete activities they perform in their daily lives. Regardless of the extent to which a human being is a conformist, any action they perform is essentially creative. Conformity is not an abstract activity; it is an action. As such, it consists of translating a kind of purpose or schema into a relatively novel human action. The repetition that takes place in the realm of nature is, to some extent, possible because natural objects are given as ready-made realities. For example, cars, dresses, and even houses are replicated because their design and the means of realizing it are determined according to established methodological principles and conditions. The same applies to processes of cloning biological organisms. But the human being is not merely a natural object: we exist in the mode of potentiality and come to life in the medium of concrete human experience. This is a continual process of creation; it resists repetition or imitation because this kind of process is individual and exists in the world as subjectivity. You can compare stones to stone, or stones to apples, but you cannot compare two or more subjectivities, although you can compare two or more modes of behavior that emanate from two subjectivities.

In practical life, we say that artists, scientists, technologists, or social reformers are creative in contrast to the multitude of ordinary people who make up the fabric of human society. This kind of characterization is exaggerated, if not mistaken, for two reasons. First, attributing the quality of creativity to what seems to be the elite of human society is, in truth, honorific; it signifies the high, remarkable, great, or genius level of their creative achievement. This type of achievement shines more than the achievements of the majority of people. However, the fact that a limited number of people shine more than the majority does not mean or imply that human beings, in general, are not essentially creative. Second, creativity is an inherent power of the human essence. Its inherence is constitutive of the essential structure of the essence and indispensable for human growth and development. Notably, a genius would not be considered a genius if their nature did not inherently possess the potential for creativity. Genius is a talent that develops under specific educational, cultural, and material conditions. The question is not whether people are or are not creative, because they are, but the *degree* of their creativity—of the extent of its cultivation and development. How many potential geniuses are hindered in the early stages of their development by ignorant, uncaring, or bigoted parents or family members? Broadly, people are not born as good, bad, angels, or devils or as artists, heroes, innovators, saints, or lovers of freedom. Similarly, they are not born as brilliant artists, scientists, or philosophers. Again, they are not born as farmers, politicians, or soldiers. They become good, bad, farmers, artists, devils, or artists primarily because the human essence is an inexhaustible possibility for realization in different ways and forms. As a power, creativity is the magical hand that initiates the process of human growth and development.

GENESIS OF THE CREATIVE IMPULSE

Any meaningful discourse about the essential nature of creation, innovation, or genius should, I propose, begin with a clear and plausible conception of "creativity" because the activity in which an object comes into being derives its nature or identity from the original, initial, or originative power that gives rise to it. The signification, meaning, or connotation of any concept is an articulation of the essential features that make up the structure of the reality it signifies. A concept or idea that does not have an actual referent is an abstract construct formed by the mind. We encounter such a construct in literary fiction, metaphysical and theological theorizing, and mysterious or extraordinary compositions. However, the phenomenon of creativity is an essential aspect of reality in all its manifestations: nature, art, science, theology, and every sphere of individual and communal experience. We cannot meaningfully and comprehensively think of any kind of reality without comprehending it as a creation or as the outcome of a creative process regardless of whether this reality is a subatomic particle, a lion, a tree, or a human being. Reality is not only a process, as Heraclitus argued. Things do not merely change; they also evolve and develop according to the laws that govern their nature. This observation is supported by the premise, which is endorsed by generally recognized metaphysical and evolutionary scientists and philosophers such as Whitehead, Bergson, Spencer, and Darwin, that the universe, viewed in its details or as a whole, is a creative advance.

This preposition may be questionable because the universe as a cosmic process, every natural object, and human life individually and communally are vitiated with upheaval, destruction, and perishing. Would this obvious phenomenon not shed some doubt about the claim that the universe is a creative advance, I may be asked. No. The destruction of an established or emerging order does not necessarily imply regress or disorder. The concept of order and advance is an anthropomorphic concept. We treat certain dimensions or aspects of nature and human experience as forms of "order" or "advance" insofar as they are comprehensible and useful. What may seem as order or progress now may not be so in the near or distant future. Broadly, disorder is the order we have not yet discovered or for some reason comprehended, and regress is the movement in nature or human experience that obstructs human development or interests. Again, what some people view as progress or advance may be viewed as regression or decomposition by others. In itself, nature is neither good nor bad, neither beautiful nor ugly. From a physical and metaphysical point of view, it is simply a process. We characterize it as creative, not only because it is evolutionary but also because the logic that underlies the dynamics of its process is essentially dialectical: creative. Although it is a judgment by the human mind, we can say that the continual emergence of different kinds of species of objects, which are indifferent to human interests and feelings, is a clear indication of advance or progress. However, this type of advance is, I think, the measure of any kind of progress in human life. It is an advance toward a higher level of order. We should always remember that in any of its manifestations, reason, whether natural or human, is essentially a form of order.

Moreover, the claim that the cosmic process is a creative advance acquires a greater measure of plausibility if we consider seriously that it exceeds in its complexity, dynamics, and possibility any other kind of reality that is an emergent phenomenon of the cosmic process. This advance is both progressive and pyramidical in the sense that it is a movement toward a higher level of perfection. This claim is based on a penetrative, comprehending, and synoptic vision of the universe as a dynamically ordered reality. For example, material reality, in its different types of formation, is higher than the phenomenon of unformed matter; botanical reality is higher than physical reality; animal reality is higher than botanical reality; and human reality is higher than mere animal reality. This gradual evolutionary advance of the cosmic process is not merely an advance but also a creative advance. It is impossible for it to evolve into higher kinds of reality if it is not inherently creative. However, although the creative impulse that energizes every individual, kind, or sphere of reality is the same, the extent of its versatility, depth, inventiveness, possibilities of realization, and dynamism varies with the variance of the material conditions under which it occurs.

CREATIVITY IN FINE ART AND HUMAN LIFE

My purpose in this chapter is not to analyze the concept of creativity in the cosmic process or in any of its manifestations in the universe as a whole but only in the domain of human life. I spotlighted the phenomenon of creativity as the essential nature of reality in the preceding section mainly to underscore the fundamental insight that the human essence as an emergent from the cosmic process is, like its source, a drop of power and that this power is a concrete manifestation of the creative power that underlies the continual creation of the universe. Creativity does not exist in it as an element or a capacity, but it permeates its totality. Like the cosmic process as a creative advance, the human being is a creative advance. Accordingly, as a drop of power, I can now say that *the human being is a creative drop of power*. How can it be otherwise if the human essence inheres as a potentiality in the formal organization of the human body and emerges from the dynamic interrelatedness of the elements that make up its structure? Can the essence that emerges from this particular kind of organization be anything but power and, more concretely, creative power? This statement is composed of two main terms: "creative" and "power." The first is the basis of self-creation, and the second is the basis of self-realization. The proposition

I shall elaborate in the following discussion is that human destiny unfolds in the process of self-creation and that self-creation is an activity of self-realization. Human living, which is the substance of human existence, is an ongoing process of self-creation, that is, of realizing the greatest possible depth of the values that emanate from the human essence. Accordingly, an authentic human being is one who lives from within, that is, from the values whose realization generates in the human individual a feeling of self-fulfillment, of being true to oneself as a human reality. The question of how I should live, love, and die is, in effect, a question of how I should live as an authentic human being. I have no right to expect from the world or any power in it more than what my nature as a human being demands or is capable of. Meeting these demands is, I submit, the ultimate source of human growth and development. As I argued in the preceding chapter, it is also the source of self-justification: Is the life I am now living, or the life I have lived, justifiable? It is justifiable inasmuch as it is authentic and authentic inasmuch as it is lived according to the values that emanate from the human essence.

It seems to me, my critic would intervene at this point in my discussion, that you tend to dilute, if not weaken, the explanatory power of the concept of creativity. Do you imply that all kinds of creativity are similar in kind and significance? You have posited one ontic locus as the fountain of all the creative processes or activities in natural and human life. A theory that explains everything in one strike fails to explain anything. I doubt that you intend to expose yourself to this charge. Accordingly, would you shed as much light as possible on the different forms of creative activity, at least in the area of human experience? For instance, does the creative act in fine art stand on equal ground with creativity in human practical and theoretical human experience, for instance, habitual acts, defending one's country in a battle, planning a vacation, delivering a lecture, composing a poem, or a symphonic work? In practical life, people differentiate between the creative activity of masters in art, science, philosophy, technology, and social reform on the one hand and the creative activity of people in personal, social, or professional experience on the other hand—is this distinction valid? In short, is there a reliable criterion for understanding the creative process in the different domains of human life?

In response to this perceptive line of questions, I can state that, ontologically, all types of creative activity derive from the creative power that initiates, energizes, and sustains the cosmic process as a creative advance.

Implied in this assertion is that the stuff that constitutes the primordial being of this process is power as a flare of creation, but it is not a blind, blank, or capricious power. It is telic in character, and the object it aims at is a particular kind of form: to be is to be a particular kind of form. A formless reality does not exist; indeed, it is inconceivable. The structure of the universe as a cosmic process is the form that embodies the complex universe as we now know it. The same dynamics apply to every emergent reality or object created by humans. By "form" I mean the essential structure of an object and more concretely, the essential features or qualities that make up its being. The formal organization of these features or qualities shines through the way they are organized. The deeper we penetrate their structure, the more we comprehend its essential nature. We cannot attribute any property to an object if it is not perceptible as an integral part of its constitutive structure. There is no need for me here to theorize on the source of this primary flare of power, that is, on whether it is eternal or created by an absolute being. Any discourse about the universe as a cosmic process is based on a reasonable understanding of its nature, which philosophers and scientists have been doing during the past three millennia.

Every emergent form from the cosmic process derives its particular nature from its source; as such, it is necessarily a creative advance. This aspect is constitutive of its essential nature. Any element of nature, be it an atom, a plant, an animal, or a human, is essentially a creative process. In all its concretizations, the differentiae of creative activity are novelty. A creatively produced object is a novel reality; the agent or originator underpinning its creation is a creative power. I can express the same point differently by saying that a novel reality comes into being *ex nihilo*, in the sense that it did not exist prior to its creation. This statement implies that the power that produced it is capable of producing an object that did not exist before its production. The medium in which it exists or acquires the status of "object" or "reality" is its form, which declares its existence and identity. Form is the language an object speaks. Accordingly, different types of objects speak different languages by the way their structure is organized, regardless of whether they are natural or human.

Moreover, form is the novel reality created by the human agent or a given natural context *qua* process. Neither nature nor the human being creates the material or substance through which the novel object is formed. Let me illustrate this point by two examples: the first from the realm of nature and the second from fine art. First, as an emergent from a certain natural environment, a particular tree is, like every other tree or plant, different from every other tree or plant by virtue of its form. Its stuff, or material, is one and the same in the totality of the botanical kingdom. If I elevate any natural process, one that brings into being a novel object the status of an agent, I can say that this process formed the material, or botanical stuff, into the form of a novel tree. Even though this stuff is an emergent process and exists as a creative process, it is nevertheless given. The creative power that presides over its creation or emergence forms it in accordance with the laws and dynamics inherent in its process.

Second, what does the artist, for example, a painter, create: an artwork? What is the stuff or medium of artistic creation? Let us spy on the artist as they are creating a work. They are surrounded by different containers of paint, brushes, a canvas, and other accessories. They mix paints in certain ways and form them into a design on the canvas. In this process, which may last a day, a week, a month, a year, or more than a year, they finalize the structure—form—of their design. They make many changes in terms of modification, deletion, or addition to the process of creating their design. The outcome is a certain representation they have created on the basis of the vision that guided the whole process of organizing the structure of the representation. A dialogue between this vision and the representation in process is active in arranging or modifying the formal organization of the elements of the representation they finally create. Now, we can ask: What did they create? The stuff, namely, the paints, is given: they did not create them; the artist used them and arranged them in a way that reflects the essential structure of the vision that existed in their mind. The only thing they contributed to the process of organizing the representation is the manner, or way, the colors and lines are formed. Although they created a representation *qua* formal organization, the reality they created is not merely the representation but what the representation symbolizes or expresses. The form they created is a kind of language instructed according to general rules, conventions, and practices approved by the art world.

Now I can state that the form of any object, be it artifactual or natural, expresses—reveals, discloses, signifies, or communicates—the nature or identity of an object. It is symbolic in character; it signifies a particular cognitive or affectional content or meaning. As such, it functions as a vehicle that conveys the content of meaning. However, the symbol can be natural, acoustic, plastic, active, religious, political, or ideological. I would not be amiss if I say that the human being is not only symbol-making but also lives in the medium of symbolic expression and realization. This assertion derives its validity from the fact that, as a formal organization, a symbol is an articulation of human meaning. The kind of meaning it communicates is embodied in its formal organization: I know what a symbol signifies or means by apprehending its symbolic organization. For example, different types of phonic formations signify or express different types of meanings, and different types of eidetic formations signify or express different types of meanings.

An important relevant remark is now in order. Is the form of an artwork conceived or imagined supervenient to the creative process? What is its status? This question merits consideration because form is the vehicle that communicates the content of meaning. The symbol is not the meaning it communicates because the meaning is an indeterminable reality and because it is apprehended immediately in the medium of intuition. I tend to think that the form the artist creates emerges in the creative process from the nature of the meaning the artist aims to express and the logic implicit in the situation that inspires the creative activity. For example, the kind of human love I express in a heroic situation is different from the kind of love I express when I attend to my sick child or when I help a friend in need in a distressful situation.

DIFFERENTIAE OF FINE ART

The degree of the expressiveness of any symbolic form is the basis or criterion by which we distinguish between fine and non-fine art: an artwork is fine inasmuch as it expresses the deepest, highest, or warmest possible meaning implicit in the values the human essence craves. Broadly, the value of any object, natural or human, is commensurate with the depth of meaning it expresses or communicates: the greater its depth, the greater its value. Expression is a mode of extrapolating or articulating a content of meaning into a symbolic form; it consists of embodying the meaning in the formal organization of the object. This process is clearly captured by the connotation of "to express." This word comes from the Latin *expressus*, a preposition of *exprimere*, "to force out."[1] The meaning that exists implicitly as an indeterminate content becomes explicit and determinate as a particular symbolic formation in the process of expressing it.

---

1. *Webster's New World College Dictionary.*

A Life Worth Living as Art

Under what creative conditions does a fine work of art come into being? An answer to this question should reveal the essence of the creative act in art and in the activity of self-realization. My answer will be based on three basic assumptions: (1) A work of fine art is cognitive in character. (2) The artwork exists as a potentiality in the formal organization if the artwork comes into being in the aesthetic experience. (3) Human depth and power of the expressiveness are the criteria by which we judge the artwork's mediocrity, goodness, or greatness.

First Assumption

An artwork is fine inasmuch as it meets three criteria: depth of meaning, universality, and test of time. These criteria are constructed on the basis of a comprehensive, penetrative, critical, and analytical examination of the nature and role art has played in the growth and development of human culture during the past five millennia. It is strange that philosophy, mathematics, religion, technology, politics, science, and politics seem to take center stage when we discuss the factors that underlie the progress of human civilization—but not art. This general tendency reflects a narrow view of the centrality of art in the development of the world's cultures, especially if we take into serious consideration that everywhere in the world, artistic expression was the first means of communication and expression. It was a fundamental source of insight, knowledge, and understanding in the rise and development of Greek philosophy and politics. The same applies to the rise of the Middle Eastern, Persian, and Far Eastern cultures. It is a mistake to think that scientific knowledge is the paradigm of human knowledge in the various areas of human experience. This type of knowledge is critical in our understanding of nature and the means of using its resources in meeting the needs of human survival, but it is not the most adequate source of knowledge of human nature and the conditions necessary for human growth and development. What if the arts of painting, music, architecture, literature, photography, sculpture, and dance were suddenly wiped out from the landscape of human civilization by a magic wand? What would human or spiritual life be like, even at present? Art is not merely entertainment, although it can entertain people quite effectively; it is one of the most powerful, versatile, and profound means of expanding our knowledge of the possibilities of human nature and human life. The mind of the artist does not imagine or create in a vacuum. Like the philosopher, their primary aim is to apprehend the meaning of existence in general and human existence in particular, and like the philosopher, they proceed in their reflection on the nature of existence from a serious understanding of the basic concepts, principles, laws, and facts conceptualized by the scientist. This knowledge is necessary for penetrating the meaning of natural and human existence, apprehending its depth, and then expressing the nature of the main questions, problems, and aspirations of human beings and hopefully promoting our understanding of ourselves and the possibilities of a better life. Did philosophers such as Socrates, Plato, and Aristotle not derive much insight about human nature and human existence from the work of the poets, dramatists, sculptors, architects, and painters who were luminaries of ancient Greek, Egyptian, and Persian cultures? Did such luminaries not play similar roles in ancient India, China, and Japan? Again, do we not derive deep intellectual and emotional understanding, or a kind of inner enlightenment, when we experience the work of artists such as da Vinci, Michelangelo, Melville, Goethe, Beethoven, Balzac, or Shelly? It is, I think, reasonable to say that scientific knowledge is the paradigm of our knowledge of nature, and philosophical knowledge of human nature is the paradigm of our knowledge of the meaning of human Ife. Although these two types of knowledge are different, nevertheless, they are organically interrelated; indeed, they imply each other. A comprehensive study of human nature reveals the limitations of the powers of the human mind in its endeavor to know the realm of nature microscopically and macroscopically. In contrast, the knowledge of the scientist is indispensable for understanding the meaning of human nature and destiny.

Second Assumption

If we cast a comprehensive and investigative look at the realm of artworks, we discover that the aesthetic object, that is, the object that comes to life in the aesthetic experience and that defines the artistic dimension of the artwork, is not given as a ready-made reality. The artwork is an artifact, an object made by human beings. We do not encounter the actuality of art in the social environment but in the medium in which the artistic phenomenon exists as a potentiality. The painting that hangs on the wall of the museum is not artwork but a representation in which the artwork inheres as a potentiality. The artwork emerges as an aesthetic object in the aesthetic experience. The representation I contemplate when I approach the painting with the intention of perceiving it aesthetically is simply a physical object to the naked eye. Its artistic dimension, which inheres in the formal organization of the representation as a potentiality, emerges as an aesthetic subject when I perceive it under certain perceptual conditions. A skillful aesthetic perceiver is one who knows the meaning implicit in the formal organization of the representation of the artwork. They can penetrate the given representation into the artistic dimension of the artwork that inheres in it as a potentiality. As I discussed a few moments ago, the artist does not create their medium; they create the way they form it. This way of organization is a kind of eidetic language, that is, thinking pictorially, acoustically, imagistically, or plastically.

Unlike the natural object, which emerges as a new reality in every moment of its processional existence, the artwork comes into being in two ways: first, as a formal organization and second, as a revelation of a novel truth. The ontic locus of the first is the artist's new form, and the ontic locus of the second is the aesthetic experience. In the first, the artistic dimension the artist creates exists as a potentiality in the formal organization of the work, and in the second, it emerges as an aesthetic object, that is, as a world of meaning. The artist is a world-maker. The world can be large or small, good or interesting, mediocre or great. But regardless of its depth, its fabric consists of human meaning.

Human meaning is essentially realized value. The reality the artist contemplates in the process of artistic creation is a dimension of the realm of values: truth, goodness, beauty, freedom, or religiosity and their derivatives. One or more values engage the reflective act in which the new aesthetic form comes into being, and the depth of the values is apprehended. The more the artist grasps the depth of the dimension of meaning implicit in the values they conceive, the deeper are the creative possibilities. The mystery and nobility of the creative in art, in contrast to the creative act in nature, is that the depth of the aesthetic object is limitless. As I argued in the preceding chapters, human values are possibilities for inexhaustible realization in different forms and ways. For example, the depth of parental love in Balzac's *Pere*, the meaning of death in Tolstoy's *The Death of Ivan Ilyich*, joy in Beethoven's *Ninth Symphony*, romantic love in Brontë's *Wuthering Heights*, the enigma of human existence in da Vinci's *Mona Lisa*, the mystery of faith in Dostoevsky's *The Brothers Karamazov*, and the tragic aspect of human existence in Sophocles' *Oedipus the King* are boundless.

The more we experience such works, the more we delve into the question of the meaning of human life and destiny.

Third Assumption

An artwork is great if it meets three basic conditions: human depth, universality, and durability (the test of time). These conditions are inspired by the fact that the realm of human values—truth, goodness, beauty, freedom, and religiosity—is a possibility for inexhaustible realization. As I argued in the preceding chapter, these values exist in the mind as schemas. As such, they signify general possibilities of realization. They denote the essential features of a type of human experience. They do refer to particular experiences primarily because (1) the human being and consequently their life is a process, and (2) the elements that make up any concrete human situation are variable. But although they are constantly changing and variable, nevertheless, they are ways of meeting peremptory needs of human survival, which are common to all human beings. Moreover, because they are schemas, human values function as guideposts that illuminate the limitless domains of the meaning implicit in their symbolic form. For example, joy is a human value. We may say that joy is a feeling of "very glad happiness, great pleasure, or delight."[2] This definition focuses on "very" and the derivatives of pleasure. Joy is a feeling of maximum pleasure or delight. But how can, or should, we define the limits of this maximum, if we can? Is it definable? Whose feeling can be the basis of a measure of a correct or adequate definition? We may say it is a profound kind of feeling. Well, "profound" comes from the Latin *profundus*, which is composed of *pro*, "forward," and *fundus*, "bottom." It is a bottomless bottom. In English, it means "very deep or low (profound abyss); marked by intellectual depth (a profound discussion); intensely felt."[3] That which is profound is fathomless. Can we say that joy is a feeling of profound pleasure in the sense of boundless or fathomless pleasure? The possibility of the limitlessness of the creation or the experience of joy stems from the fact that, as a type of value, it signifies a profound depth. But this depth is human depth; it is not a discrete event in the life of the human mind. For example, penetrating into the depth of the human dimension in Beethoven's Ninth Symphony is in effect penetrating into the depth of the human dimension of a human being: I move into the world expressed by

---

2. *Webster's New World College Dictionary.*
3. *Webster's New World College Dictionary.*

this symphony. Do all the people who experience this symphony penetrate the infinity of the joy Beethoven expressed and embodied in the score of this symphonic work? Of course not. Again, as we delve deeper into it, do we better experience and learn how to move into the world it embodies? It is common among literary teachers and ordinary people to say that we discover new and deeper meanings when we experience artworks in later years in life—why?

We delight in the experience of the deepest possible aesthetic dimension of artworks primarily because they are worlds of human meaning, that is, of realized values. Enjoyment of human meaning is not only the nutrient of the human mind but also the greatest source of human satisfaction. We become our true selves when we sizzle in the kind of fire we feel when we are enlightened, are graced by our friends, perform an act of goodness for a stranger, experience reverence for the Absolute, pray with a genuine feeling of piety, or lose ourselves in works such as Shakespeare's *King Lear*, Mann's *The Magic Mountain*, or Raphael's *School of Athens*. In our theoretical and practical lives, we pursue aims, goals, or purposes—whether personal, professional, social, entertainment, aesthetic, political, or moral—why? I tend to think that the driving force of this pursuit is craving a kind of meaning. Absence of meaning in our lives is the ultimate source of anxiety, boredom, loneliness, and cynicism. We tend to lose our sense of life when we lose our sense of meaning. Let us not forget that the building blocks of human character, or differently the "I" that presides over the course of our lives, are realized values. If we take into account this fundamental fact, we can immediately see why the quest for meaning is the substance of human life and its realization the substance of human destiny.

At the beginning of this section, I stated that an artwork is great inasmuch as it expresses human depth, endurance, and universality. Now I can add that the artwork is enduring in the sense that it stands the test of time, is universal, in the sense that it speaks to all human beings, and grand inasmuch as it is expressive of human death. However, the expression and communication of human depth, which is a depth of human meaning, is the primary criterion in our attempt to evaluate not only works of art but also human action.

CHAPTER FIVE

Artistic Creation and Self-Creation

SELF-CREATION

I have so far submitted, elucidated, and defended four main propositions. First, as the source of the manifestations in the world, the human essence is an emergent form of the cosmic process. Although it emerged from a physical reality and exists as a potentiality in the formal organization of the human body, it is not reducible to physical or material terms. The primary impulse of this essence is an impulse to human life. As an integral element of the body, this impulse is thrust into existing in the world as a human reality. Second, as a potentiality, the human essence inheres in the human body as a power that can be concretized as a complex reality. The essential structure of this power consists of three basic capacities: thinking or intellect, affection or feeling, and volition or willing. They comprise the essential structure of human nature in the sense that any discourse about any dimension of the human phenomenon either refers to or expresses a feature of the human essence. Third, as a potentiality that inheres in the human body, the life of the human being consists of realizing, or concretizing, its three basic capacities; it is a realization of the powers that make up the structure of these capacities. This objectification emanates as a human flare from the core of the realization. Fourth, the constitutive capacities of the human essence exist as urges or drives whose fulfillment is achieved by meeting peremptory needs inherent in the human impulse to life. The basis for meeting these needs comprises five primary values: truth, goodness, beauty, freedom, and religiosity. Living according to these values is

Artistic Creation and Self-Creation

a necessary and sufficient condition for the possibility of human survival. These four propositions imply that a person's life is human inasmuch as it is a vivid and comprehensive realization of these values. Accordingly, because life is a process, it follows that it is a continual process of growth and development. Living this kind of life is the substance of human destiny.

Moreover, I have argued that a life of growth and development is a fine work of art. Such a life is an artistic creation, the way a work of art is an artistic creation. An authentic human being lives in accordance with the five values that emanate from the human essence. This kind of life is complete or fulfilled; more importantly, it is worth living and justified because it is worth living. The criterion for evaluating the artistic dimension or status of a life is *human depth*: a human life is a fine work of art inasmuch as it is lived from the utmost depth of the values that emanate from the human essence, or put differently, inasmuch as it is lived authentically. In developing my argument, I analyzed the structural analogy between the life and vocation of the human individual and the life and vocation of the fine work of art. Both the artwork and the human individual come into being in the mode of potentiality. The first inheres in the formal organization of the artwork the artist creates, and the second inheres in the formal organization of the human body. The first derives its being from the reality of human values that exist as possibilities of inexhaustible realization in different ways and forms, and the second derives its being from the same realm of values. The life of a human being, or that of the artwork, is valuable inasmuch as it embodies the greatest possible measure of human depth. This analogy implies that both the human being and the fine work of art are value realities in the sense that their essential structure consists of realized values. Accordingly, the value of a human life or an artwork is measured by the extent to which it exists in the world as a living flame of the human essence.

You seem to blur, if not erase, the demarcation lines, if there are some, between mediocre, good, and great art on the one hand, my critic would object, and mediocre, good, and genius human beings on the other. You have argued that the artwork, like a human life, is mediocre, good, or excellent inasmuch as it is a profound human depth. But can we distinguish among "mediocre," "good," and "great" art and human lives? Moreover, there is a clear and, I think, radical difference between the artwork and the human being. The first is a created object, and the artist is its creator. The artist determines the human depth of the work. The second is a self-created object—who determines its depth? I raise this question because you have pointed out that the "who" of this question is beyond the limits of human understanding. Can we view human depth as a criterion of evaluation if we do not know these limits? Is the analogy between a human's life and vocation and an artwork's life and vocation not shaky and can it not be used as a principle of explanation?

First, from the fact that the artwork is a created reality and human life is a self-reality, it does not necessarily follow that they are not or cannot be structurally analogous. In fact, they are. First, both initially exist in the mode of human potential; second, the building blocks of their structures are human values; and third, both come to life in the medium of human experience as meaning. The human essence is indeed given, but it is not given as a ready-made reality. On the contrary, it is given as a potentiality. Even the potentiality is a created reality. It emerges from the womb of the natural process the way an artwork emerges as a potentiality from the womb of the human mind. It may seem strange to recognize that the realization of the artistic dimension of the artwork is an act of self-realization—why? Because it does not exist in the world as a concrete reality. The aesthetic experience I undergo in the process of perceiving an artwork aesthetically is mine. I am its author and am one with it when I have the experience. It is important to remember that an analogy is not a relation of identity but a conceptual framework that functions as a principle of explanation. Its purpose is to illuminate a complex problem or reveal a mysterious aspect of a particular human reality. Let me explain in some detail the explanatory function of this analogy.

First, the aesthetic experience is, as I indicated earlier, a world-creating experience. The texture of this world is human meaning. I leave the world of ordinary life, which is social, personal, professional, or cultural in character, and move into the world the artist has created as a potentiality. This world expands in its dimensions the more I proceed into the depth envisioned by the artist and ingressed in its form. The world that opens up in my experience is the handiwork of my imagination. I become one with it, and it ceases to be the world the artist created exclusively because it is brought into being by my mind and because the stuff of which it is made is the stuff of my mind. Even though its structure comes from the artist, it gets baptized and transformed into a new identity by the hand of my mind.

The aesthetic experience is a moment of self-realization and, as such, a moment of self-creation. How? The mind, which acts as a subject that presides over the process of constructing the world implicit in the artwork as a potentiality, is a concrete, developed reality in process. Every moment of its existence is a thrust into the next moment. Its preceding state of being ceases to exist the instant it passes into its succeeding state of being. However, although the preceding state of being ceases to exist or passes into the realm of nonbeing, its essential structure endures into the next or succeeding state of being but as a new reality. The new reality keeps the essential identity of the preceding state of being as a more abundant and developed depth of being. Why? The world of meaning that unfolds in the experience of the perceiver, and which is constructed creatively by their intellectual and imaginary resources, becomes incorporated into its developing structure. This incorporation expands their intellectual, affectional, and volitional capacities. The mind emerges from this experience as a new reality. For example, suppose I have an aesthetic experience of an artwork such as Sophocles' *Oedipus the King*. When I penetrate the intricacy of the psychological dynamics that underlie Oedipus's relation with his father whom he killed, his mother whom he married, and his children who were his brothers and sisters, when in this process I linger on his relation with the blind yet wise man Tiresias on the one hand and his idealism, absolute respect for the truth, courage, exceptional skill in government, and willingness to bow before the judgment of justice on the other—yes, when I visit the alleys of this world, interact with its dwellers, contemplate the domain of its beliefs and values, especially when I delve deep into the profound human depth of its world in all its triumphs, failures, blunders, defeats, and struggles, can I remain silent or a mere spectator? Indeed, the world that unfolds in my experience is my world when I am having it. Am I not a witness and a participant in what happens in it? Am I not a witness to its truth? Can I dismiss it as entertainment, a time-killer, or a trivial event in my life? On the contrary, do I not grow in self-understanding and in understanding nature, the creative possibilities of the human essence, and the meaning of human existence?

It is, I think, reasonable to judge *Oedipus the King* as a great artwork not only because it is an expression of a profound human depth but also because it is universal and enduring. First, although ontologically it emerged from the bosom of an ancient culture and embodies its beliefs and values, it speaks to human beings in different cultural orientations everywhere in the world in the present and over the past three millennia. The characters are vivid instantiations of the human essence. We identify with them. We think, feel, and act the way they think, feel, and act. Who would not admire

Oedipus for his courage, respect for the truth, superior intelligence, and love of his family? Who would not revolt when he kills his father, marries his mother, and begets children from her? Who would not sympathize with him when he agonizes over his blunders and later plucks his eyeballs from their sockets? Who would not pity him when he suffers unto death and curses the day he was born? Who would not cringe when he commits a capital crime soon after he kills his father and marries his mother? Alas, who would not wish that some devil or angel would intervene to stop him from committing his crimes? Does Oedipus not personify the possibilities implicit in the human essence in its passion for life, love, truth, glory, tragedy, magnanimity, baseness, frailty, genius, and folly? Does the drama delivered in this work not represent the struggle of people in their endeavor to grow and develop in their humanity?

Although I may not be an Oedipus, although I may be an ordinary human being who is alive to the radiance of the human essence in their heart and mind, can I be and feel the same after I live the human pulse of the aesthetic world that unfolds in my experience of this dramatic piece? On the contrary, do I not feel enlightened, different, more substantial, and more in touch with myself when I emerge from its world and move into the world of practical life? Living in this kind of world, which is short and imaginary, is not and cannot be an occasion of amusement, diversion from the routine, or appearing to the social world as a sophisticated human being but an occasion for a direct encounter with myself and feeling my inmost being; it is an existential response to the call of human growth and development. This is the kind of call Socrates made to his fellow Athenians when he repeatedly reminded them that the unexamined life is not worth living. A serious work of art is a source of inspiration, self-understanding, and an invitation to celebrate the rite of human living.

Second, despite the fact that all human achievements change, and most of them pass into the world of oblivion sooner or later, the good, the true, and the beautiful endure primarily because they are the human essence writ large. The human essence does not exist apart from its concrete manifestations in the world. As I argued in the first chapter, its mode of existence in the world is potentiality. As such, its existence is abstract. The artwork endures. Its endurance is relative to the endurance of the human essence; that is, it endures as long as the human essence endures primarily because they are a concrete realization of peremptory needs. Put differently, the human essence thrives in and through its realizations in the world.

Artistic Creation and Self-Creation

How can the artwork endure if the cultural language in which it is written changes and gradually passes away, my critic would suddenly ask. As you have discussed, *Oedipus the King* was written in a language that does not exist anymore, yet it seems to speak to human beings today—how? What makes works such as *Oedipus the King* endure? We can also ask, what makes the true, the good, and the beautiful, the free, and the religious endure? It would seem paradoxical to say that perishing is king in the universe and, at the same time, hold that human values endure. Can you resolve the mystery of this paradox?

The key that unlocks the door of this apparently lies in the fact that, as an impulse to human life, the human essence endures. However, let me hasten to add that it does not endure as a particular, concrete, or specific reality but as a potentiality in the formal organization of the human body. The basis of its endurance or any of its manifestations is the endurance of the values that exist as existential responses to peremptory needs inherent in its essential structure. First, these values exist in the artwork as potentialities awaiting realization in the aesthetic experience; this mode of organization is the mode of a schema whose structure consists of the general or universal features that constitute the identity of any of its realizations. They do not exist in the schema as finally defined or articulated features but as possibilities for inexhaustible realizations in different ways and forms, which depend on the kind of aesthetic perceiver who undergoes the experience under certain perceptual conditions. This aspect of the artwork entitles it to the status of "living" reality or organism, which in turn entitles it to the distinction of having a career. It enables the work to be experienced, interpreted, and evaluated differently in different cultural or situational conditions. The basis of this entitlement is the dynamic nature of the human essence and, from its inmost and, more concretely, inherent craving for human existence.

The peremptory needs inherent in the human essence and the values that emanate from these needs hang in the ceiling of consciousness as guideposts and as appropriate equipment by which the mind intuitively apprehends a perceptual content and subsumes it under the essential structure of a schema. For example, the way the Athenian people experienced, interpreted, and evaluated *Oedipus the King* in the fifth century BC was different from the way the Romans in the first or third century AD did, and different from the way the Europeans in the Renaissance did, and still different from the way the peoples of the world do today. What endures in this and similar cases is the universality of the work and the endurance of its essential structure as a *human schema*, that is, the values that express the fundamental craving of the human essence. Otherwise, how can we as Chinese, Americans, Russians, Arabs, Kenyans, or South Africans experience this artistic masterpiece as a world of human meaning that pulsates with tragedy, greatness, glory, creativity, rationality, on the one hand, and weakness, frailty, limitations, and the folly of human nature, on the other hand?

THE AESTHETIC EXPERIENCE AS AN EVENT OF SELF-CREATION

The realm of fine art is an astonishingly large domain of human reality. This domain, which exists in the human mind as a magnificent garden of human achievements, represents one of the most significant concretizations of the human essence: the beautiful. The impulse to create, enjoy, and live in the medium of a beautiful environment is innate to the impulse to human survival. Even though we do not dwell on this domain in a world overwhelmed by the demands of an unusually complex web of social, religious, political, economic, cultural, and survival forces, it is, I think, a central sphere of human growth and development. In all its concrete manifestations, the built environment is a shining recognition of the constructive power of the impulse to human life: architecture, technology, human institutions, science, philosophy, and the whole artifactual world. Let's stand on a hill that overlooks this world, which is constantly changing in complexity and refinement, and cast an evaluative judgment on it as an embodiment of human culture. We shall be bound to view it as a fine work created by the communal mind of humanity. My eyes would relish the beauty of the streets, buildings, libraries, art centers, shops, gardens, landscapes, monuments, and kinds of technological works; it would also relish the striking interweaving of the remarkable institutions, organizations, associations, and the intricate social formations within which people conduct the business of living. I suggest this possibility of viewing the human world not only to emphasize that the craving for beauty is an impelling force of human nature but also an indispensable medium of human self-realization.

We cannot, in this context, either marginalize or ignore the possibility of viewing nature as an object of aesthetic experience, not only in the sphere of the garden or architectural landscaping, which are human creations, but also in the open vistas of the forest, the valley, the mountain, and the plain. Although we cannot identify the infinity of aesthetic formations in nature, I can assert without a shred of doubt that natural formations can be experienced aesthetically, mainly because (1) human beings possess an aesthetic sense, and (2) some of these formations may, in principle, delight the imagination. An aesthetically cultivated mind can apprehend the dynamic interrelatedness of the elements that make up their structure. Does it matter whether a human or a superior mind or power constructed or created them? Do I need to know the author of works such as *Oedipus the King*, *Doctor Faustus*, the Ninth Symphony, *Hamlet*, or *Mona Lisa* to appreciate them aesthetically? In contrast, do we not understand and appreciate aesthetically literary, pictorial, or sculptural works of anonymous authors of past cultures? That which is beautiful does not exist in nature as a discrete reality. The source of the beautiful is the human essence. Many people cannot perceive, much less experience, the beauty of the boundless artworks that populate the world's cultures—why? Is it a lack of aesthetic cultivation? Of course, but what is aesthetic education if it is not the education of the aesthetic sense that inheres in human nature as a potentiality? Moreover, what if this sense is but a power that exists as a peremptory demand of the human essence?

Moreover, it is possible for a learned mind, one that is knowledgeable of the basic principles of the sciences and the humanities and the dynamics of human life, to comprehend the structure of the universe *qua* cosmic process in its details as an ordered whole, to penetrate their inner forces and workings and comprehend, in a synoptic vision, the presence of the power that animates this mind-boggling universe. It is plausible that this universe is creative and telic in character. Can the human race survive in it if it is not telic and ordered? How many mystics in the cultures and religions of the world have made this kind of spiritual adventure? Does it not underlie the metaphysical systems that punctuate the history of philosophy? Is it not the foundation of the major religions of the world? Again, on the ground of practical life, do we not enjoy a beautiful sunset or sunrise? Do we not delight in the Grand Canyon, Niagara Falls, or the tranquility of a prairie illuminated by the silver rays of the moon on a midsummer night?

I made the preceding remark to accentuate the significance of the aesthetic experienced as a peremptory need and an essential medium of human self-realization. Whether in the realm of fine art or nature, the act of self-realization is an activity of self-creation. The human being creates themselves as the individual they aspire to be from the core of the values of truth, goodness, beauty, freedom, and religiosity. The value of beauty is the focus in this part of my discourse. Now, in what sense is an act of self-realization an activity of self-creation? What does the human being create in this activity? Let me at once propose that they create themself as a human reality. I assume that they do not create their body, although they attend to its needs, because it is an integral part of the natural process. The domain of self-creation is the domain of the "I," the self or subjectivity, which is the unity of the totality of the experiences one undergoes in the course of one's life and which comes to life as "an individual" in the form of a subject that presides over these experiences. As I argued earlier, this subject is conscious of the world around them and self-conscious in the sense that they can introspect their inner being; that is, they can examine and evaluate the *intellectual, affectional, and volitional* activities. In this type of experience, they discover that they are the agent who owns their experiences and that they are their source. They sees themself in their experiences, and they see them as parts of themself. As mental states, they pulsate as the thread of their life. I have emphasized "intellectual, affectional, and volitional" because they constitute the pillars, indeed the building blocks, of themself. They are structural owners or hands that perform the activity of self-realization. The self that acts in the performance of an action is the unity of these capacities. The self emerges from this unity. I assume in this analysis that the self is not a metaphysical or psychological entity but an activity in process. Every moment of self-consciousness is a moment of a living experience in process, whether significant or trivial, long or short, or practical or theoretical, conscious, subconscious, or unconscious. A self that is not an experience in process does not exist as a concrete reality in the world.

Accordingly, the medium of self-realization is an experience in which the primary values are its source and substance. The realization of value in an experience implies an ingression of a new reality in the mind of the acting subject. This ingression is not an activity of storing new content in a drawer of the mind because there are no drawers or enclosed spaces in it but the realization of the value as an integral part of its structure. Once realized, the value becomes infused in the mind as the unity of its intellectual, affectional, and volitional capacities. The mind as a whole grows in depth in the act of self-realization. A realized value signifies the creation and incorporation of the realized meaning in the thinking and feeling mechanism of the mind. This activity is expansive in character; it deepens and widens the powers of the mind in its function as a thinking, feeling, and willing faculty. It is the defining aspect of self-creation on the one hand and human growth and development on the other. But the self that creates itself is, as I have emphasized repeatedly, a process. As such a process, its self-creation is also self-recreation. In addition to creating itself by the ingression of values in the structure of their mind, thereby emerging as a new reality, it also renews its existence in every process of its existence. Although its preceding state of being ceases to exist, its essential structure lingers in the succeeding state of being. This is a necessary feature of the logic of process, or change. It is impossible for anything to change, and consequently to be a process, if it does not become different from itself, and it is impossible to become different from itself if it does not acquire new qualities or relinquish some of the qualities that has made up its structure or identity. Again, "process" is inconceivable intellectually and ontically if an object in process does not move from its present state of being to its succeeding state,

However, unlike natural objects, which are given as ready-made realities and governed by the laws of nature, the human being is not given as a ready-made reality. Every new state of being they move into is essentially an activity of creating a new being *ex nihilo* and recreating themselves as a particular reality. The body in which this new reality is recreated happens according to the laws of nature, but the human dimension that constitutes the structure of the human self is recreated according to the logic and laws inherent in the human essence. Its inherence in the human body is the basis of its continual recreation. I exist in my body. Although it remains the same *in principle*, in the activity of living, I grow and develop as a human individual. In this activity, the body in which I exist is humanized because it functions as the medium of expressing and objectifying my being as mind, and because the human essence inheres in every fiber of its formal organization. I have emphasized "in principle" because, as a natural reality, my body changes and ages according to the laws of nature: I see myself as an individual in and through my body, and I see my body as a part of my being as human integrity.

The point that merits special emphasis at this juncture of my discussion is that human values are the foundation of self-realization, self-creation, and self-recreation because they are what is constantly created and act as the basis of my enduring identity as a human being. Their range and depth are the source of creative activity, not merely in the mode of biological survival but especially in the mode of human survival. The extent to which a human being creates and recreates themself in different ways depends on the extent to which they maximize the depth implicit in the values of truth, beauty, goodness, freedom, and religiosity, that is, the extent to which their life is a maximal realization of these values. This fundamental insight should, I think, be not only the theoretical but also the practical aim and practice of education.

Any serious activity of self-realization involves a plethora of human values, although one or a few may figure prominently depending on the kind of situation in which a person acts. We do not exist in the world as intellects, affectional capacities, or decision-making faculties but as an interactive unity of these faculties, which act as a subject. Moreover, the life situations that constantly emerge in the course of our daily practical life are complex and involve more than value. Some are more central. Accordingly, it is inconceivable for a person to undergo a pure, intellectual, affectional, or volitional experience mainly because they do not exist in the world merely as intellects, affectional capacities, or volitional faculties. Every action we perform involves the totality of our being. This fact lends support to the claim that every human experience we undergo is an experience of self-realization. Even a minor experience, such as a vacation, shopping spree, or walk in the park; reading a novel; or playing with our children involves a diversity of values and takes place as an experience of self-realization.

A work of fine art, especially a masterpiece, is one that presents a substantial slice of human life, a mosaic of human values. This mosaic may be large or small, simple or complex. It comes to life in the aesthetic experience as a world of human meaning. This kind of experience is, as I have indicated, an instance of self-realization because it offers an occasion to live in the medium of a symphonic spectacle of realized human values. It is frequently created as a microscopic representation of a macroscopic vision of a critical dimension or aspect of human life. This world does not unfold in my mind as fiction but as a living stream of human experience, nor does it unfold as a reality external to my mind but as an integral part of my being. It does not unfold spontaneously or passively but as a creative act of my imagination. It is creatively made because it comes to life in my experience and nowhere else. As I argued earlier, the artist does not create a ready-made reality but a potentiality to be realized by the aesthetic perceiver in the medium of the aesthetic experience. The activity involved in this kind of experience is constructive in that my capacity for thinking, feeling, and willing expands in depth. Every activity I perform in this process extends and augments the limits of these capacities. Let me illustrate this essential aspect by revisiting *Oedipus the King*.

This artwork is a dramatic exhibition of the fundamental human values—truth, beauty, goodness, freedom, and religiosity—in action on the stage. The primary value that dominates the action that gradually unfolds before my eyes on the stage is a *tragedy* as an instantiation of the primary value of beauty. Every other value surges as a living pulse in the unfolding of the world Sophocles envisioned during the process of artistic creation. They surge as an organically interrelated web. I do not perceive or respond to the interweaving of the impact of these values philosophically or scientifically but as a flame of aesthetic fire—as a human flame, as a flare of humanity, as throbs of the human essence. This flare, which ignites as the action unfolds step-by-step, reaches a high point of intensity when Oedipus discovers the capital crime he unwillingly, yet willingly, committed—yes, this fire enables me to see this synthesis of human values in conflict as an embodiment of a valuer of the tragedy of human existence.

I sizzle in this fire while I am watching the play mainly because during this time I am in its world and because I am one with it. Does such a fire not enliven every fiber of my being? Does it not transform those fibers into deeper, stronger, and more intense flames of fire? But when I leave this spiritual adventure, contemplate it in the privacy of my soul in my bedroom, and examine the amazing thread of action that led Oedipus from moment of his birth to the moment of his fall, I cannot but reflect on the meaning of human existence in general and my existence in particular. Can I, in such a state of reflection, remain silent? The drama I have witnessed and in a way lived is a kaleidoscopic representation of the dance of human values on the stage of human life—of the passion for self-realization.

The dance of human values, whose stage is the mind and heart of the human individual, is the highest expression of the passion for love of life. It is the centerpiece of the rite of human living. This assertion may strike my reader as an overstatement, but it is not. Does the love of life not underlie every action we perform, every serious project we design, and every goal we hope to realize? If we grant, as we should, that these and similar activities are projected by desire and knowledge, what makes these and similar activities worthy of desire or pursuit? If we critically and objectively examine the source that animates them, we discover that it is human values. When the fire of these values fades, the luster of joy in living fades. Joy in human living is commensurate with the extent to which the life of the human individual is a shining example of the values of truth, goodness, beauty, freedom, and religiosity. Does the feeling of joy in our minds and hearts not diminish when we are idle, lonely, oppressed, old, disenfranchised, or deprived of the opportunity or possibility to realize the diversity of human values in our lives? Again, do we not feel elated when we implement a project we designed, perform an act of love to a fellow human being, undergo a mystical experience, read a serious book, or discover a new truth?

SELF-REALIZATION AS AN ART

If we contemplate the historical landscape of human societies as communities and individuals, my critic would wonder, we observe a remarkable difference not only in the level of self-consciousness as human beings but especially in their responsiveness to the peremptory needs of the human essence. These values reached a high degree of articulation and conceptualization in the recent past. I tend to agree with your thesis that the human essence is common to all members of the class of *Homo sapiens*, but living consciously, thoughtfully, and purposefully from the values that emanate from its structure is a newly born consciousness. Did the people of various cultures who lived prior to the Renaissance not live from the essence of human values? Even today, as discussed in the previous chapter, do all the people of the world live from the human essence? No. What strikes the mind of an astute social reformer is that human societies from the earliest period of human civilization to the present are hierarchical in their structure. The scale of the hierarchy ranges from mediocre or dilettante to the great or the best. Following Pythagoras, Plato vividly encapsulated this feature of human reality in his classification of human societies into three classes: rulers, defenders of the state, and producers. The first class is distinguished by wisdom, the second by courage, and the third by temperance. This is an elitist conception of human nature. However, this conception has, ever since his day, undergone a variety of interpretations, modifications, and criticisms theoretically and practically. If the human essence is one and the same in all human beings, why do people in even contemporary advanced societies not live from the fiber of the human essence that is supposed to flare in their hearts and minds? Why should the human essence flare differently in different people individually and communally?

An answer to this question has distinctly and insistently been on the minds of philosophers, social reformers, artists, religious leaders, serious politicians, and thinkers, and it looms prominently at the forefront of this discourse.

I aver that the human essence does not shine equally or with the same intensity individually and communally in the world's different societies. I also aver that this flare has been growing in its intensity in different ways in different parts of the world during the past six millennia. Moreover, it is possible that this difference will prevail for a long time to come. The primary difference for this diversity is, I propose, the availability of the material, cultural, educational, and social resources and conditions necessary for exuberant human growth and development. However, the key to an understanding of this reason is the primary fact that the human essence exists as a potentiality in the formal organization of the *human body*. It may seem paradoxical if I add that human survival is a necessary condition for the possibility of biological survival. As one of my biology professors remarked in one of his lectures when I was at university, the human body cannot think creatively, love creatively, and make sound decisions creatively—much less live creatively—if its stomach is hungry or if it cannot protect itself against the adverse forces of the environment. But, in contrast, how can the human body survive biologically if the human being does not think creatively, love creatively, and make sound decisions creatively? One can ask whether necessity is the mother of invention; accordingly, does the need to survive not impel the human mind to think, feel, and act from the depth of the human essence—rationally and creatively? I am inclined to think that the human and biological dimensions of human survival logically and ontologically imply each other. If this is the case, and I think it is, the question we should consider seriously is, under what necessary and sufficient conditions can human beings live and flourish from the human essence?

These conditions differ from one society to another, one individual to another, one historical period to another, and one geographical environment to another. This difference should account for the realization of the human essence differently in the different parts of the world. The fulfillment of these conditions is developmental. For example, the realization of the functions of the human mind—perception, conception, relation, assertion, imagination, comparison, evaluation, and speculation to mention a few—is not easy. They emerge, grow, and develop in refinement and practice the more the intellect develops skills in the various areas of intellection and the more the mind explores the possibilities of realizing its functions as a constitutive element of the essential structure of the human essence. If we reflect on the progress of the domains of human civilization in the course of its historic development, we discover that this course is not only admirable but also a testament to the creative powers of true human essence. We may begin this process of reflection in the elemental constituents such as shelter, tools, education, art, defense, industry, religion, means of communication, and transportation, and focus on the gradual emergence of the agricultural, industrial, and computer revolutions. A historico-philosophical mind that scrutinizes the struggle, hardships, courage, vision, failures, successes, and unyielding will to survive at the human level would undoubtedly recognize the boundless creative resourcefulness and power of the human essence in its effort to assert its impulse to human life. This kind of mind would also acknowledge that biological survival is concomitant to human survival. The more we develop as a race and expand our horizons of thinking, feeling, and willingness, the more we expand the scope of material and spiritual living. The remarkable advance of the sciences, art, philosophy, and politics during the past five hundred years, which culminated in the most impressive achievements of contemporary technology, is clear evidence of the boundlessness of the creative power of the human essence.

Although brief, the preceding remark about the historical development of the living reality of the human essence during the past several millennia is to lend support to the propositions that (1) regardless of their level of development or whether the quality of their lives is primitive, mediocre, good, or excellent, human life is a process of creative responsiveness to the peremptory needs inherent in the human essence or, put differently, the primary impulse to human life; (2) the depth of the realization of this impulse depends on the material, social, cultural, and spiritual conditions in which an individual, a community, or a society happens to thrive and (3) and the life of the human being is an ongoing process of growth and development from the values that emanate from the human essence. An understanding of any dimension of human life and the conditions of its development, slumber, retardation, or perishing should either assume or be based on a clear and reasonable conception of the human essence because it is the locus of the logic and dynamics that underlie the realization of any human experience. This is why this book begins with a conception of human nature (or human essence). The assumption that lends warrantability to this methodological step, which I discussed in the first chapter, is that knowledge of the source, initial state, or cause of an object is not only critical but also a condition for knowing its nature because the object derives its being and existence from it. The relation of a cause to its effect is especially efficacious in our attempt to understand the relation between the human essence and the life that emanates from it. The process of emanation is an essential extension of its being. In this case, the cause exists in potency in its effect, and the effect expresses the nature of its cause.

As my analysis in the previous chapters makes clear, the human essence exists in the formal organization of the human body. I have repeatedly conjoined "human essence" with "formal organization of the human body" because the body is the medium in and through which the human being exists as a human reality. This existence emerges when the rising youth, in whom the human essence exists as a potentiality, becomes conscious of themselves as an independent being, that is, as a subject at the peak of adolescence. The transformation of the body into a human body begins with the emergence of self-consciousness. It marks the process of realizing the human essence into a human individual. It is the most serious and momentous event of the activity of self-creation; it sets the grounds for any future acts in the process of growing and maturing. Why? Even though it emerges gradually, one's life project is painstaking and sometimes adventurous. It may last a long or short time, depending on the social, cultural, and educational norms and conditions in which the rising thrives. Every future choice or action, which is to a large extent creative in character, will originate from this design. The more it is built on a firm and human foundation, the greater the range of creative possibilities.

CONDITIONS OF SELF-CREATION AS AN ART

Given the present state of human development, under what conditions can the rising youth construct a life project that expresses their inherent sense of value, way of living, talents, and understanding of themselves and the world around them? Philosophers, sociological scientists, and social reformers frequently wonder about the "who" or the kind of identity an adult or a young person is. This is not merely a theoretical but also a practical question because an essential urge of the human psyche is an urge to be "somebody," that is, to be recognized, accepted, and appreciated as a human individual, as a particular identity. The source of this urge inheres in the womb of self-consciousness. Only a self-conscious being demands to be recognized, respected, and appreciated as an identity. The premise that underlies this urge is that a subject *qua* particular identity is not given to the world as a ready-made reality but as a personal achievement. It deserves respect, acceptance, and appreciation because it thrives in the world as a living flame of human values and because self-transcendence is an impelling force inherent in the human essence. This force is the basis of "sociality" or "being with the human other." It is, moreover, the basis of the forms of social existence: family, friendship, and social association. It is a requisite for the possibility of thriving as a human individual.

The question of the conditions of constructing or developing a life project or design is, at bottom, a design whose realization would *maximize* the greatest possible measure of human self-realization in the world. I emphasized "maximize" because the question is not merely the realization of human values, for the modern state provides the structural conditions for self-realization, but the most significant possible depth of these values. The question is to be able to forge one's way as an authentic being in a world dominated by vain glory, selfishness, naive individualism, economic power, success, superficial hedonism, and especially the stringent and sometimes cruel struggle for human survival.

Moreover, how can the rising youth choose their individual identity? This question stems from the inmost core of human subjectivity. When I discover myself as an independent human being, I also discover that I do not have an identity. Suppose I stand before the mirror of truth and ask myself, "What kind of individual do you desire to be?"

A voice answers my question: "I desire to be myself."

"But I do not have a self. How can I choose myself?" I plead.

"You are a potentiality to be any identity you desire to have. You have been a member of your society for about fifteen years. You can choose to be a farmer, teacher, engineer, lawyer, doctor, businessperson, artist, preacher, devil, angel, dilettante, gangster, or nurse. Remember, choosing your identity is in effect choosing a way of life."

"I understand your response," the image in the mirror retorts with a quivering voice. "What you say is reasonable, but the question that disturbs me is how to act according to what you say on the ground of reality. This kind of experience is a first for me. I do not yet possess the skill in making this kind of choice. When I reflect on myself as it is in its present state of consciousness and try to imagine the being I desire to be, I find it difficult to grasp, much less to command, by an act of vision, who exactly I am in the next hour, day, year, or the distant future. In this state, I find myself standing before a closed door. I cannot envision the best way of

Artistic Creation and Self-Creation

living in this world. If I understand you correctly, every action I perform is an activity of self-realization, which takes place according to an idea or a plan. How can I choose the right principle for my actions and means of implementing them?" This plain yet profound question reveals the logic of creative activity.

With an equally quivering voice and concerned eyes, I spontaneously respond in the following manner: "Regardless of whether they are critical, momentous, or hard, and regardless of whether they are habitual, routine, new, or accidental, all the actions we perform in the course of our daily lives originate from the concrete situations that unfold in the medium of our social, professional, religious, personal, or cultural existence, which is always contextual. The circumstances of our individual lives, which are occasioned by complex and different factors, conspire to create the situations we find ourselves in. They initiate the need to act. These needs are, in turn, aroused in our minds an immediate consciousness of the appropriate values and beliefs in terms and on the basis of which we respond to the situation. The life of a human being is a stream of experiences. The bed of this stream is time. We are drops of time, and we exist in time. Every activity we perform happens within this seam. This fact of human life is a necessary demand to act creatively: first, because our lives are constantly a thrust into the future of which we are, in principle, ignorant and second, because our being is a process of unfolding into the future. For example, I am delivering a lecture on the nature of justice to my students, which is an activity in process taking place in time. The door of the lecture room opens slowly. The dean's secretary stands with pursed lips and two serious eyes demanding my attention. The students' eyes abandon me and move toward the door. Solemn silence reigns supreme in the lecture room. I stop my lecture and walk toward the secretary. "Your wife had a heart attack. She was taken to the emergency room twenty minutes ago. The dean thought you should know as soon as possible," the secretary said in a sad voice, leaving without adding anything further. The question that jumped into my mind was this: What should I do? How should I act? How can I make the right decision? I have an obligation to serve my students and the college. I have a responsibility to love and care for my wife. The dean did not give me permission to dismiss my class and join my wife at the hospital immediately. Will the students suffer badly if I leave the class? The factors that make up this situation are common to most, if not all, the social, professional, or religious situations we find ourselves in throughout the course of our practical lives.

Some are consequential and make a big difference in our lives, and some are ordinary and make little difference. But no matter the degree of their significance, formative impact, or the degree of their significance, they are occasions of self-realization and consequently self-creation.

We can identify two distinctive levels, kinds, and moments of self-creation: the first is primary, and the second is derivative. The first is the source of the conception, or envisioning, of the design of one's life project, and the second is the source of the identity of particular activities people perform daily in their endeavor to survive. The first serves as a purpose or plan of action, and the second serves as a principle of action. The first is the basis of one's identity, and the second is the source of the identity of the different kinds of activities we perform. However, both derive their being from the human values that emanate from the human essence. Let me elaborate on these two moments of self-creation in some detail.

First, what kind of creative activity is involved in conceiving one's life project, purpose, or vocation? This kind of activity necessarily emerges with the emergence of self-consciousness in the rising youth. Prior to this primordial event, the young person does not have a personal identity; they are a social identity. It is ingrained in them by their family, school, and social environment. The "who" of their being, or identity, is not chosen by them but given as a "gift" by their benefactor: society. The beliefs and values and their way of acting do not originate from their mind, although they exist in their "social mind" because their mind has not yet emerged as an autonomous faculty. It exists as a potentiality in the formal organization of their body that is ready to emerge into the world of light as a living drop of human existence. But although they do not exist as an autonomous mind, they possess the conceptual and affectional material and equipment they received in their social growth and development to act as an autonomous human being. The burst into being of self-consciousness rises from the bosom of the self that is ingrained in the psyche. They stand on the ground of this self when they face themself in the mirror of truth and simultaneously feel the itch aroused by the call to be an identity. How do they respond to this call?

The social environment does not give them only a temporary identity but also the intellectual and practical skills to create a new one. First, the structure of any identity they choose will emanate from the fundamental structure of the human essence and, more concretely, from the depth of the values that shine from this essence. This is a gradual, developmental

Artistic Creation and Self-Creation

process. "I want to be me!" or "I want to be the subject that presides over the creation of my own identity. The life I choose to live should be based on the values that will function as its building blocks." Reflection on the domain of human values is, I think, the first step in conceiving or designing a life project or a life vocation. This reflection implies that the kind of life one chooses should be based on these values. Second, the domain of reflection in the endeavor to choose a life project is the institutions and organizations that make up the fabric of society. As I argued in the first chapter, the unity of these institutions, which make up the state as a political formation, is human nature writ large. Their structure is founded on the values that emanate from human essence. They are the existential medium in which people thrive as human individuals. Moreover, they reveal what human beings can do.

The activity of choosing one's vocation in life does not happen in one act or sudden revelation but evolves gradually. Broadly, the process of its evolution begins during adolescence. It proceeds as a quiet, intuitive, and existential dialectic between the young person's reflection on their inmost desires, capacities, talents, inclinations on the one hand and reflection on the ocean of professional possibilities society offers on the other. I characterized this process as an "existential dialectic" because it gradually emerges in the midst of experience, trial and error, counsel, inspiration, and emulation of a distinguished or successful citizen. Any design of a kind of vocation a person chooses is not, practically speaking, a philosophical act of speculation by an intellectual, dispositional, and value-laden activity. Moreover, frequently it is not articulated as a clear or final principle of action or as ways of acting and organizing one's life but as a nucleus, a vision, or an ideal. It grows in clarity of structure as one advances in life achievements. The identity of a human shines through the main activities and achievements they contribute to society in general and in their immediate environment in particular. Broadly, we know a person's identity by what they do in the world, not merely by what they think or feel about themself.

A necessary condition of the possibility of choosing and maximizing the depth of the individual's self-realization is passion—intense desire and love of the vocation or way of life one chooses. If the activity of realizing oneself originates from their mind and heart, if it is an existential response to the impetus to human life, if they feel that their life is their dearest passion, it would follow that passion is the animating power of the activity of their self-realization. We should never forget that the process of self-realization is the source of satisfaction the human mind craves. The intensity of the passion we feel in pursuing our life projects is an expression of our love of life. Its depth is commensurate with the depth of the values we realize in the vast medium of personal, social, moral, religious, professional, and personal experiences.

The second level, or moment, of self-creation is the totality of actions we perform in the course of our daily living in the spheres of experience: social, professional, and cultural. These spheres constitute the medium in which we realize or create ourselves. The thread of experiences we undergo in this medium is the thread of self-creation. What is the basis of this creation? We can distinguish two bases. The first is personal and primary, and the second is institutional or cultural. The basis of the first is principles, rules, or standards derived from the values of truth, goodness, beauty, freedom, and religiosity. They are the foundation of the different kinds of intellectual, moral, aesthetic, religious, and individual experiences we undergo in different situations. Although they are distinguishable for the purpose of analysis or identification and communication, more than one value is involved in the actions we perform daily. Values do not exist discretely or singly in practical life but as a web. Even though particular actions derive their identity from the ingression of one primary value, such as justice, elegance, or piety, they entail other values. For example, one can say that every significant action we perform in the course of daily living, regardless of whether it is religious, social, or intellectual, is essentially moral, and every moral or aesthetic action we perform also involves religious, social, intellectual, and other types of derivative or primary human value. Any act of self-realization in any domain of human value is a realization of the whole self. The self is the unity of its actions; accordingly, any action affects every constituent of its being. Do I not grow as a whole when I undergo a religious, aesthetic, or moral experience?

The second level, or moment, of self-creation involves activities in the different institutions of society. These are cultural or social in character. Their basis is not rules, principles, or standards directly derived from human values but customs, traditions, conventions, norms, practices, and recognized traditions such as weddings, funerals, birthdays, and social or religious festivities. But although they are not directly based on articulated moral rules, principles, or standards founded in human values, they are nevertheless expressive of the sense of value that inheres in human essence. They are occasions of self-realization. The human being is not a machine, and human life is not mechanical but a flame of human life. The human is, as I repeatedly emphasized, an inexhaustible possibility of realization in different ways and forms. Regardless of whether it is a genius, a profound feeling of joy, an explosion of scientific or artistic creation, a romantic union, or a heroic action, it does not happen according to established rules, criteria, or principles but originates directly from the core of the human essence as an impulse to human life. However, its origination does not take place as a spontaneous eruption but arises from the living presence of realized values in the sphere of one's society or the realm of human civilization. In all its manifestations, this realm is the human essence writ large.

PRINCIPLES OF THE ART OF HUMAN LIVING

You have elucidated the dynamical structure of the activity of self-realization and vehemently argued that self-realization is an activity of self-creation, my critic would now ask with two impatient eyes. You have drawn an analogy between the creation of a fine artwork and the creation of the human self. Both come into being *sui generis*. In both types of creation, the basis of the "fine" aspect of the creative act is the expression or realization of human depth. The deeper the depth, the greater the artwork. Similarly, the deeper the activity of self-creation, the deeper the self-realization and consequently human satisfaction. Authentic human life is a profound instantiation of the values emanating from the essence. Moreover, you have made a distinction between skill and fine art. We learn the fundaments of a skill in human survival in the process of social growth and development. But human survival at its best is living from within, that is, from the values that emanate from the human essence. This kind of life is viewed as fine art in contrast to the life of the indolent, the drifter, the conformist, or the person who is contented with a mediocre way of living.

The thesis explained and defended here is that authentic human giving is a fine art. If it is, one wonders how one learns this art. The critic continues, you have lamented the fact that we stuff the mind of the rising youth with a large volume of theoretical ideas in physics, mathematics, biology, archaeology, chemistry, history, economics, philosophy, theology, business, communication, law, and agriculture, but we do not teach them how to lead an authentic way of living. Your lament is based on the fundamental premise that we do not live to know, but we know to live well. Therefore, teaching the rising youth how to lead a life worth living should be the centerpiece of education. What are the principles of this education? How can one cultivate the art of human living? Or, what does it take to show the rising youth how to move from the skill of living to the art of human living?

I shall begin my answer to this question by stating that education is the method needed for transforming a skill into an art and, more importantly, into a fine art. What are the principles of this method? Any effective, plausible attempt to answer this question should, I think, proceed from an adequate concept of education. A quick look at the theory and practice of education during the past three millennia will show that this concept is shrouded in a maze of conflicting interpretations, understandings, practices, and views. However, I shall base my discussion of the elements that make up its structure on my experience teaching philosophy in a liberal arts institution for forty years and extensive research in the philosophy of education. I shall begin with a concept of and then expand its implications in my exposition of its application in the art of the human living sphere.

The word "education" comes from the Latin *educatus*, a preposition of *educare*, "to bring up, rear, or train." *Educare* is derived from *e*, "out," and *ducere*, "to lead." Broadly, it means "to train or develop the knowledge, skill, mind, or character, especially by formal schooling or study."[1] Socrates enunciated the fundamental principle of education of character in the fifth century BC: learning is self-learning. The learning implied in this enunciation aims at self-understanding, that is, knowing the essential elements and powers of the human mind. This knowledge is indispensable for living a worthwhile life. Accordingly, the aim of any educational authority, institution, environment, or person, whether theoretical or practical, should be to lead the student (or adult) to know themself. Acquiring knowledge both of nature and human nature is a means to self-knowledge because we are integral parts of the human and natural world. The knowledge acquired in school or university is, in general, theoretical, but it is the torch that illuminates the terrain of the human self. The task of the educator is to show—lead, train, coach, or guide—the learner to use this torch in examining themselves and discovering the powers, impulses, needs, desires, or cravings that constitute their inner being. The education process, be it individual, collective, or institutional, is not a process of dictation, that is, of indoctrination, but of teaching the rising youth how to open the door of their minds and discover what makes them tick as human beings. Stuffing the mind with ideas with the intention merely of memorizing them or

---

1. *Webster's New World College Dictionary*.

acting on them passively, uncritically, or thoughtlessly closes this door of the mind and undermines its autonomy and the impetus to growth and development. Acquiring ideas is a necessary but not sufficient condition for the possibility of education. They are a means to an end, and the end is to understand oneself. This end is the basis of action. They perform this function when they are transformed into instruments of self-understanding. I assume, in making this observation, that knowledge is power; it empowers the mind to think, understand, and choose soundly. The task of education is to infuse the ideas the student learns or thinks with life, with the power of the truth they signify and with the capacity to feel this truth in their personal life experience. The high road to this kind of education is a method of questioning, critical thinking, analysis, inspiration, and most of all, being a vivid, living example of a growing, developing mind. This principle applies to learning in the humanities and sciences and professional education. If I am to express this point metaphorically, I can say that the task of the educator is to show the rising youth, by words and deeds, how to be spies of the human mind, which involves opening its door and observing its mental states: ideas, beliefs, feelings, emotion, capacities, desires, and especially its possibilities. A direct, dialogical encounter with the diversity of these elements is the best possible means of comprehending the meaning and significance implicit in them, especially the roles they play in the life of the growing individual. An idea is not a lifeless, inert mental state that sits on a shelf of the human mind. It is a moving power of the human mind. It is a potential drop in human understanding. This understanding serves as an impetus to rational decision-making.

The articulation of the principles of education for human living should proceed from the assumption that the rising youth possesses functional skills in the art of survival. This skill is a necessary condition for the cultivation of the art of human living. Young people acquire this skill during the period that culminates in the peak of adolescence. During this period, they learn most of the basics of how to meet their biological, social, personal, and psychological needs. They also learn the fundaments of their intellectual, affective, and volitional action. The question that looms existentially in their consciousness is, how can I be me? This question stems from the impulse to human survival. As I remarked a moment ago, choosing their identity is an open-ended process. The cultivation of the art of human living should begin immediately following the emergence of self-consciousness in the minds of rising youth, who are transitioning from their high school mentality to a rational one. The knowledge they receive during this period is decisive for learning the art of human living. It is also central to an intuitive comprehension of the principles and ideas of the sciences and humanities. Their worldview grows in depth and breadth from the kind and extent of the knowledge they acquire in this period of their growth. Usually, the ideas, skills, and habits they develop when they are young take a strong hold on the structure of their minds. Directly or indirectly, they view themselves and the world around them from the standpoint of these ideas, skills, and habits. This is why an education for the art of human living should begin early in the life of youth.

However, the cultivation of this art in the early period of human growth and development is urgently needed because it is a necessary condition for choosing one's vocation or life project. I cannot but spotlight a widespread practice in education in general, namely, the tendency of some parents, teachers, advisors, and even friends to coerce, pressure, or influence youth in a most loving and caring attitude to choose a certain way of living or vocation, as if they know the mind and heart of the youth, as if they know the secret of human nature, as if they know the secret of human life. They seem oblivious that the urge to exist and thrive in the world as an autonomous being is a primary impulse in human nature.

CAN ART BE CULTIVATED?

It is, I think, important to remind my reader that the cultivation of an art is generically different from the cultivation of a skill. The first takes place according to established rules, conventions, practices, and a margin of ingenuity, which are learned by observation, experience, or reading certain manuals. The logic of the first is derived from established practice, and the logic of the second is derived from a vision, conception, or design that originates as a practical response to a given problem or situation. What the rising youth needs is not a continuation of a way of life instilled in them by their family and the immediate environment but the creation of a new self or a new way of living *sui generis*: How can I create myself out of the large stock of knowledge and experiences I have undergone on the one hand and the intellectual, affectional, and volitional skills I learned in the process of my development until the present moment on the other? The self that exists as a potentiality in the formal organization of the body exists as a subterranean layer of being. The emergence of self-consciousness endows this potentiality with the power to speak! How can the self create its language in the process of its continual growth? This process is a creative activity, and the self that emerges gradually comes into being as a novel reality.

With the help of parents and cooperation with educational authorities, high school education should respond to this call. How? I recommend establishing a program as a requirement for college or university students' graduation that focuses on the ideas and principles of the art of human living. Its primary aim would be to explain in theory and practice how to translate the basic ideas and laws of the sciences and the humanities into principles, criteria, or standards and ways of making practical decisions based on these ideas, standards, and principles. It is prudent to avoid theory as much as possible, mainly because the student has a sufficient theoretical background. Instead, the emphasis should be on the logical dynamics of decision-making, that is, on how to think wisely in difficult or problematic situations. Analysis of particular cases, literary or artistic illustrations; discussion of models of ways to act; and evaluating problems that reveal the relevance of the various kinds of knowledge the student learned during their high school and college or university education should expand their understanding of value situations that emerge in the course of their daily lives. Explanation, illustration, depiction, and exhibition should replace lecturing, dictation, and memorization. Moreover, realistic engagement and personal confrontation in the context of evaluating concrete situations should be prominent during the program. The instructor should step down from their pedestal or role as a professor, mistress, or master and act as a collaborator and indirectly as a guide the way Beatrice guided Dante in *The Divine Comedy* from the dark alleys of hell to the gates of heaven or the way the music teacher shows their student how to transform the musical core into a living musical event that transcends the score. Broadly, two principal types of activity should predominate in this program: the first is imitation, using illustration, depiction, analogy, and the second is engagement, utilizing actual participation in the evaluation of concrete problems or situations. No matter their academic background, the teacher cannot teach their student directly how to be an artist in human living because learning a skill is different from learning how to be an artist. The teacher cannot teach their students how to be an artist the way a farmer can teach their child how to be a farmer but rather the *conditions* for becoming an artist. Some conditions are inspiration, hints, suggestions, personal confession, constructive observation—especially to be in touch with one's mind and heart—and the need to express one's feelings, ideas, emotions, or vision.

A primary condition for learning how to be an artist is knowing oneself—one's beliefs, values, desires, strengths and weaknesses, and image of oneself on the one hand and knowledge of the essential values, beliefs, and level of cultural development of the environment on the other hand. An artist is a lover of human beings, and an artist in human living is a lover of human life. A lover is a passionate heart and mind. Passion is the driving force of the creative act; it is the soil that nourishes this kind of act, and it is also the source of the capacity to express and influence its beneficiary constructively. An act that issues from the mind and heart is more believable, communicative, and meaningful than an act done mechanically or robotically. Passion is the source of the radiance that emanates from the human essence. It is, moreover, the source of the power that animates the activity of self-realization. It is important to emphasize that passion is not a blind, capricious, or fitful gust or outpouring of the mind but an emanation of the impulse to human life. For example, there is a big difference between a teacher who delivers their lesson with their lips and placid face and a teacher who delivers it with their soul and body, that is, with their eyes, hands, legs, lips, and vibrant voice. And there is a big difference between a piece of music that is a perfect rendition of the score and one that is an exuberant flare of power, joy, love, or tranquility. An artist in human living is a passionate lover of the beautiful, the true, the free, and the religious. But, alas, how can one be such an artist if the flare of life does not spring from the values that constitute the foundation of their being? How can the life of a human being be authentic if it is not an objectification, that is, realization, of these values?

Contemporary society tends to emphasize expertise. For example, teachers in philosophy are experts in a certain area of philosophy, a major philosopher, a school of philosophy, or a certain period of historical development. Doctors are expected to be experts on the function of an organ or a part of the human body. We can observe this tendency in computer science, law, business, banking, chemistry, biology, engineering, architecture, political science, sociology, and other human inquiry and practice domains. Although it is commendable and should be encouraged, for it represents an unusual advancement in our knowledge of nature and human nature, this new phenomenon of compartmentalization is gradually creeping into the lives of human beings to the extent that their lives tend to revolve around one main type of human experience, namely, the area of their expertise or profession, without paying sufficient attention to their needs as human individuals. They tend to allow themselves to be reduced to social or professional "functionaries" as if their destiny or vocation in life is to be such functionaries, as if they are born to be lumps of clay to be formed in the image of this or that function, as if the human essence that cries for fulfillment in their minds and hearts is a negligible itch or nuisance. I am not in any way critical or opposed to the cultivation of expertise in human experience; on the contrary, this development is laudable, for it is indicative of the advancement of human knowledge and self-understanding. I am critical of reducing human beings to the realization of the mediocre and one-sided dimension of growth and development. Moreover, I am critical of the commodification, or functionalization, of human beings into modes of being that merely serve ideological, political, or idiosyncratic agendas.

One central objective of the program I am proposing is to spotlight three distinct modes of consciousness. First, the purpose of the different types of knowledge achieved during the past five millennia is not to receive a college degree or assume a certain social, political, or professional status but to provide the conditions for self-understanding. This kind of understanding is not only useful but also a requisite for designing and cultivating one's vocation in life. Second, the different academic subjects the student explores, including their academic major, are interrelated, and their basis is knowledge of nature and human nature. These disciplines imply each other. Knowledge of the fundamental ideas and principles of the types of knowledge in the sciences and humanities is necessary for an adequate self-understanding and, consequently, for planning the course of one's life in the world. Third, human destiny consists of the activity of self-realization, and self-realization consists of the realization of the values that emanate from the human essence. As an echo of the commonly known dictum, human beings cannot live by bread alone but also by the spirit that resides in their hearts and minds. The stuff of this spirit is human values. Only when we recognize the insight of this wisdom in words and deeds can we realize our destiny or vocation in life. A one-sided, one-dimensional life is a life with one eye, one ear, one leg, and half a will. It is lame, although it thrives and enjoys a few morsels of human satisfaction now and then.

The members of the committee who conduct the learning adventures of this program should be living models in the art of human giving, and they should represent the major sciences and humanities objectively. I say "adventures" because the classes or workshops they conduct should be structured as occasions for inquiry, critical reflection, ideas, and questioning life problems. The purport of this statement is intellectual discipline: focus. Well-roundedness of personality as an ideal, no matter its idealism, should always hover on the fringe of the conversations and discussions. From a methodological point of view, it is desirable to exemplify the Socratic spirit of interaction with students. This exemplification should spring from the signification of Socrates's plea: "Care for your soul!" In this context, it is worth remarking that this enigmatic philosopher lived by the beliefs and values he sought to communicate to his fellow Athenians. He studied the sciences, philosophies, arts, mathematics, and cultural achievements of Greece. His mind was encyclopedic in its scope of theoretical and practical knowledge from Homer's day to his. He was convinced that the quest for knowledge is a means to an end, and the end is the perfection of the human soul. He was a teacher of the art of human living by the way he taught and lived. Is it an accident that Plato's early dialogues, which are known as Socratic, are devoted to an analysis of fundamental values? Is it an accident that the method employed in conducting these analyses continued in their breadth and depth in the remainder of the major dialogues?

Lest I expose myself to a possible misunderstanding, I should emphasize that the program I propose is not a "capstone" program that marks the highest achievements of the sciences and humanities, or the inherent interrelatedness between them, but the intimate relation and critical relevance of the types of knowledge of human life.

It is difficult to construct a general syllabus that functions as an organizational model of the program, not only because the academic, financial, and teaching resources of colleges and universities vary but also because the conditions of human life everywhere in the world are constantly changing. The syllabus of such a program should, I think, originate from the structural constitution of the academic program of every institution of higher learning. However, despite this existential situation, I can suggest some general thematic titles that may be useful in organizing its activities. These topics may be considered implicitly or explicitly, depending on the wisdom of the curriculum panel that designs the program.

First are the elements or features that define the human dimension of the human being, namely, intellect, affection, and volition. What is the nature of these elements? How do people respond to the needs they create? A critical discussion of these elements should serve as a general framework for the analysis of any significant question about the meaning of life. Second are the basis, origin, and place of human values in human life. What are these values? How do people view them? What makes an object, purpose, activity, or aim valuable? More importantly, what makes realizing these values the basis of a happy life or a life worth living? Some values, such as freedom, honesty, or love, may be considered in some detail. Third is the meaning of human destiny: Why do we exist on the face of the earth individually and communally? Human life is short: How should we live it? What does the idea of "human destiny" signify? Are we the authors of our destiny? Fourth, what is self-realization? How is it related to human living? In what sense are the actions we perform creative? What is creativity? What are the conditions for cultivating the art of self-creation among the rising youth? Fifth, how are the types of human knowledge in the sciences and the humanities that the students have learned relevant to their lives? Here, the concept of decision-making should figure prominently. Accordingly, how can these ideas inform, illuminate, or help one make practical decisions in the different areas of their life? Sixth, what is individuality and its relation to autonomy? Can a selfish person be a human individual? What is selfishness? These general themes are not final or finally articulated, nor are they comprehensive in their scope. They are suggestive of the kinds of conversations that may be conducted in the proceedings of the program.

Suggested References and Bibliography

Altshuler, Thelma, and Richard Janaro. *The Art of Being Human*. London: Longman, 2005.
Appa, Margaret. *The Science and Art of Being Human*. New York: George Ronald, 2024.
Aristotle. *The Nicomachean Ethics*. Oxford: Oxford University Press, 1980.
Berdyaev, Nicolai. *The Destiny of Man*. New York: Harper Torch, 1960.
Brenner, John. *Life Within: The Art of Being Human*. N.p.: Create Space, 2018.
Coslett, Papa Joe. *The Art of Being Human*. Bloomington, IN: Trafford, 2023.
Campbell, Caroline. *The Power of Art: A Human History*. Whitewright, TX: Pegasus, 2024.
Epictetus. *The Art of Living*. New York: HarperOne, 2007.
Frankl, Viktor. *The Doctor and the Soul*. Boston: Beacon, 2014.
Hạnh, Thích Nhất. *The Art of Living*. Read by Edoardo Ballerini and Gabra Zackman. New York: Harper Audio, 2017.
Hegel, George W. F. *Hegel's Philosophy of Right*. Oxford: Oxford University Press, 1952.
Fromm, Eric. *The Art of Loving*. New York: Harper Perennial, 1956.
McNamara, William. *The Art of Being Human*. N.p.: Papa Moa, 2018.
———. *The Art of Human Adventure*. Mishawaka, IN: Better World, 1991.
Marcel, Gabriel. *The Philosophy of Existentialism*. New York: Citadel, 1970.
———. *The Mystery of Being*. South Bend, IN: St. Augustine, 2001.
Mercer, Mary. *The Art of Being Human*. Buffalo, NY: Prometheus, 1997.
Muhammad, Imani. *The Art of Living*. N.p.: Moueix, 2023.
Ortega y Gasset, José. *Man and People*. New York: Norton, 1963.
Plato. *The Collected Dialogues of Plato*. New York: Pantheon, 1961.
Proctor, Bob. *The Art of Living*. Slatington, PA: Jeremy Tratcher, 2015.
Rose, Michael. *The Art of Being Human*. Brooklyn, NY: Angelico, 2022.
Sartre, Jean-Paul. *Existentialism Is a Humanism*. Hoboken, NJ: Prentice-Hall, .
Sri, Edward. *The Art of Living: The Cardinal Virtues and the Freedom of Love*. Zeeland, MI: Ignatius, 2021.
Tillich, Paul. *Love, Power, and Justice*. Olympia, WA: K. S. Pope, 1980.
Whitehead, Alfred N. *Process and Reality*. New York: Macmillan, 1978.
Webster's New World College Dictionary. Newly updated edition. 5th ed. Boston: Houghton Mifflin Harcourt, 2016.
Wilfred, Peterson. *The New Book of the Art of Being Human*. New York: Simon and Schuster, 1962.
Wilkenson, Michael. *The Fine Art of Being Human*. N.p.: Three Points of Contact, 2018.

Index

Aesthetic Experience, 108, 112–115
Aristotle, 8, 38, 77, 102
Art, 7, 73, 81, 96
Artwork, 109–112, 116
Axiology, 102–105

Bacon, Roger, 11
Bacon, Francis, 12
Balzac, Honore de, 102–103.
Beethoven, Ludwig van, 102, 103, 104, 105
Brahe, Tycho, 11
Bronte Emily, 103
Built Environment, 36, 41
Buonarotti, Michelangelo, 102

Character, 17
Civilization, 23, 25
Community, 44–47
Constitution, 43–48
Copernicus, Nicolas, 11
Cosmic Process, 4
Creative Impulse, 94
Creativity, 90–96
Cura, 70,

Darwin, Charles, 11, 95
Da Vinci, Leonardo, 72, 102, 103
Democracy, 43–45
Descartes, René, 11
Divinity, 67
Dostoevsky, Fyodor, 103
Doubt, 75, 77
Education, 37–40, 128, 130
Expression, 100
Existential Dialectic, 125

Fine Art, 107, 112
Finitude, 58

Galilei, Galileo, 11
Goethe, Johann von, 102

Hegel, Georg W. F., 20
Heraclitus, 27
Human Essence, 2–3, 13–15, 50, 54, 65, 110
Human Depth, 100, 104, 107
Human Destiny, 71
Human Embodiments, 18–20, 39
Human Living, 129–130
Human Nature, 8–10, 54,

Importance, 30
Impulse, 18, 25–28, 67
Individuality, 44–49, 65–68

Kepler, Johannes, 11
Lavoisier, Antoine, 11

Mann, Thomas, 105
Meaning, 12, 18
Melville, Herman, 108
Mind, 1, 13, 48

Newton, Isaac, 11

Peremptory Desires, 59, 55
Peremptory Needs, 29, 55, 104, 132
Phenomenon, 14
Plato, 2, 9, 28, 54, 102, 118, 134
Potentiality, 18–20, 50
Power, 51–52, 67

Index

Preamble, 43
Pythagoras, 118

Raphael, Raphaello Santi, 105
Russell, Bertrand, 12,

Schema, 39, 57, 80
Science, 11, 12
Self-consciousness, 15, 48
Self-creation, 6, 47–49, 85, 105, 121
Self-realization, 6, 29, 85, 108
Shakespeare, William, 105

Shelly, Percy B., 102,
Skill, 83–86
Socrates, 89, 90, 102, 134
Solitariness, 62
Sophocles, 103, 109
Subjectivity, 16, 17–19, 21

Tolstoy, Leo, 103
Value, 29, 30, 33, 41, 43

Whitehead, Alfred N., 12, 27–29, 52, 53, 95

www.ingramcontent.com/pod-product-compliance
Lightning Source LLC
Chambersburg PA
CBHW072152160426
43197CB00012B/2346